D0984870

Chicago Day Souvenirs

CHICAGO DAY
UNITED STATES OF AMERICA
COLUMBIAN HALF DOLLAR

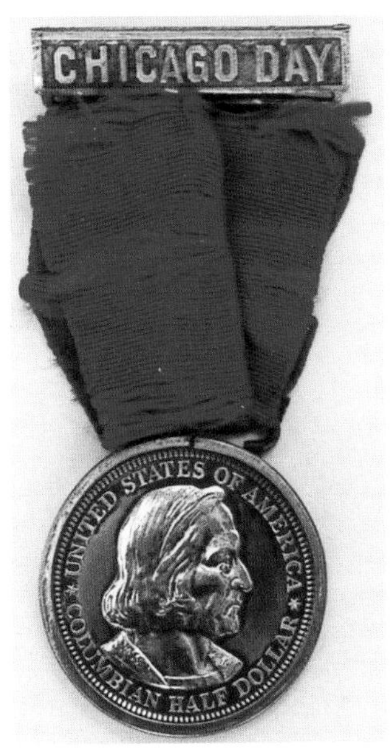

The Chicago Day Badge

(Actual Size)

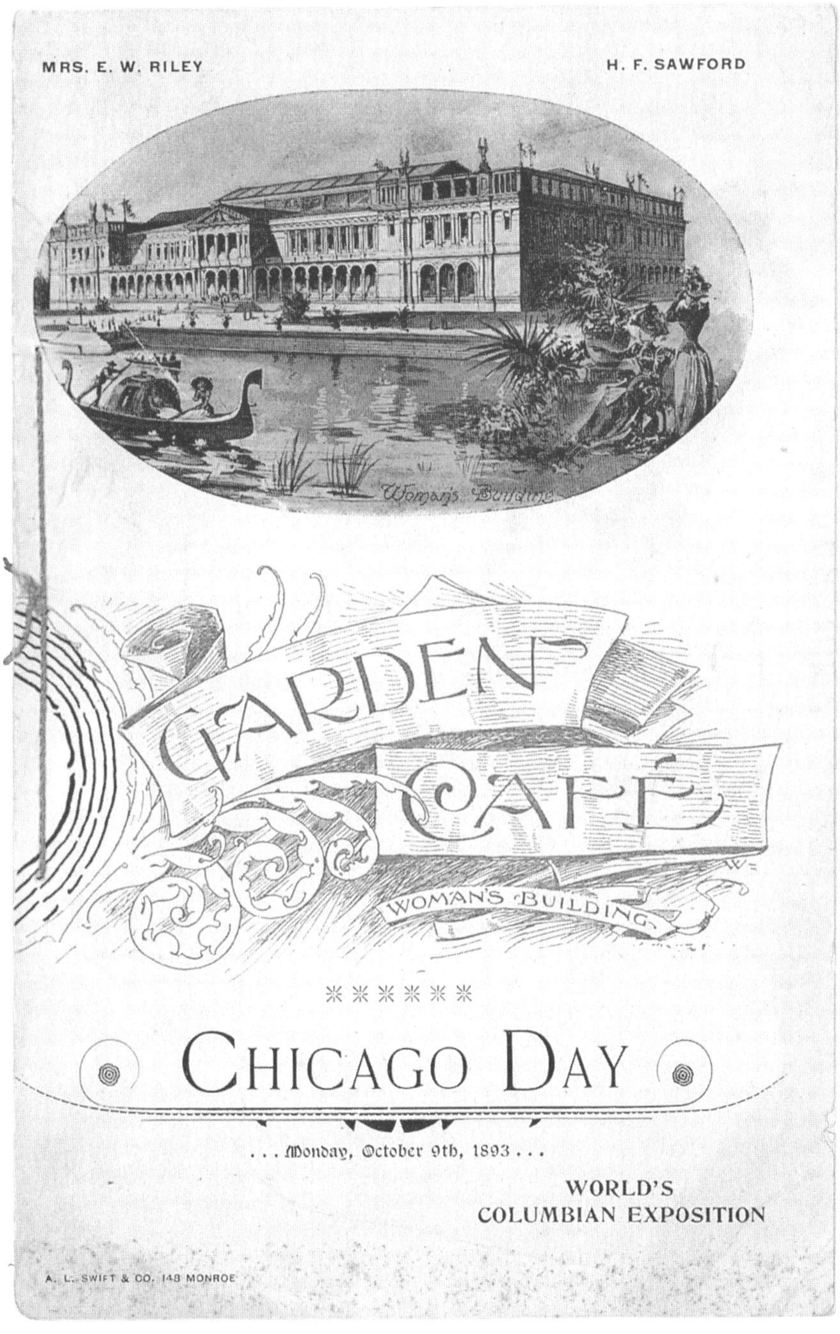
MRS. E. W. RILEY
H. F. SAWFORD
Woman's Building
GARDEN CAFÉ
WOMAN'S BUILDING
CHICAGO DAY
. . . Monday, October 9th, 1893 . . .
WORLD'S
COLUMBIAN EXPOSITION
A. L. SWIFT & CO. 148 MONROE

Chicago Day Special Menu from the Woman's Building (Actual Size)

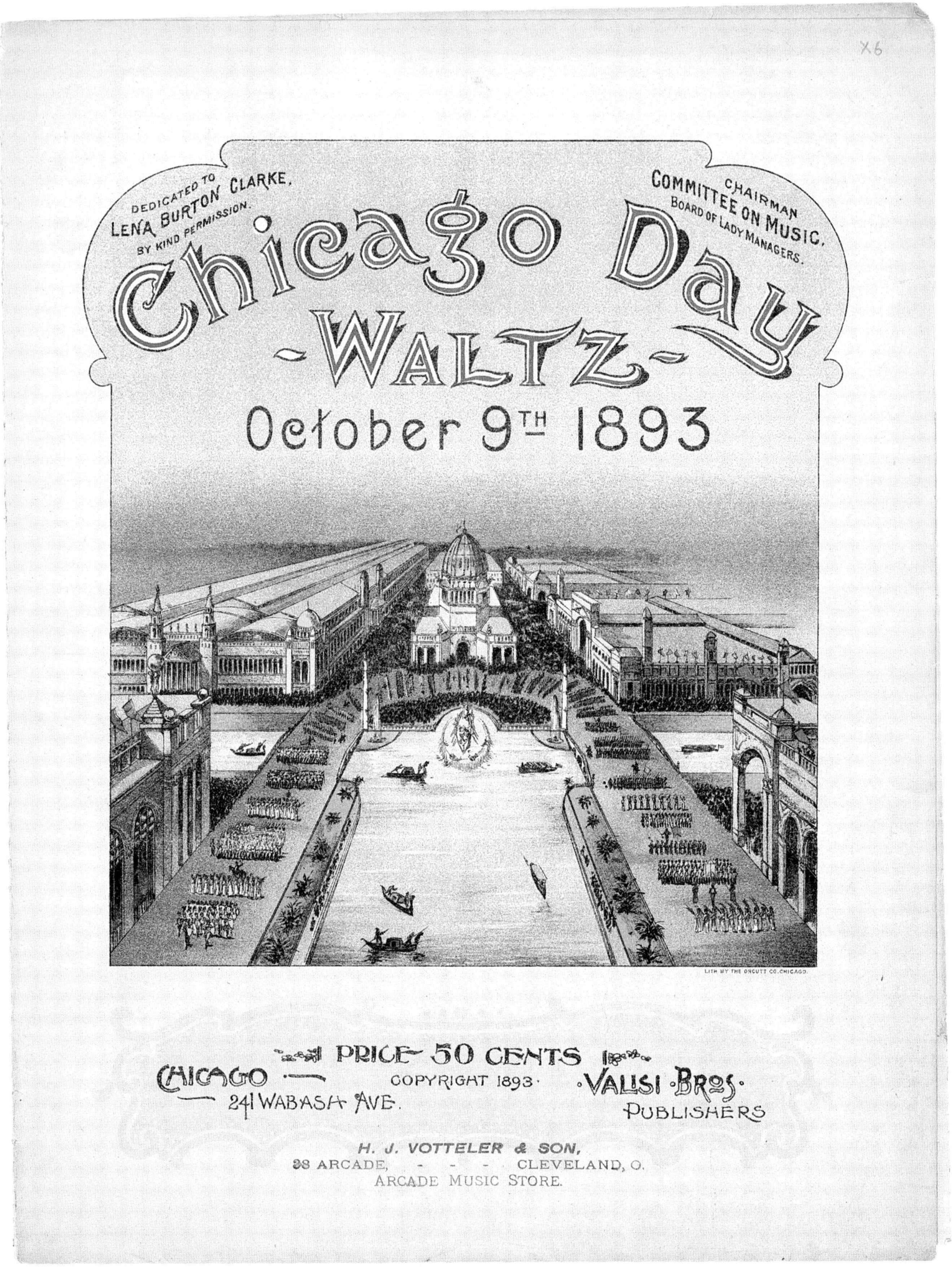

Dedicated to
Lena Burton Clarke,
By kind permission.
Chairman
Committee on Music,
Board of Lady Managers.
Chicago Day
-Waltz-
October 9th 1893
Lith by the Orcutt Co. Chicago.
Price 50 Cents
Chicago
Copyright 1893.
Valisi Bros.
241 Wabash Ave.
Publishers
H. J. VOTTELER & SON,
38 ARCADE, - - - - CLEVELAND, O.
ARCADE MUSIC STORE.

Sheet Music Commemorating Chicago Day (Original size, 14 by 10¾ inches)

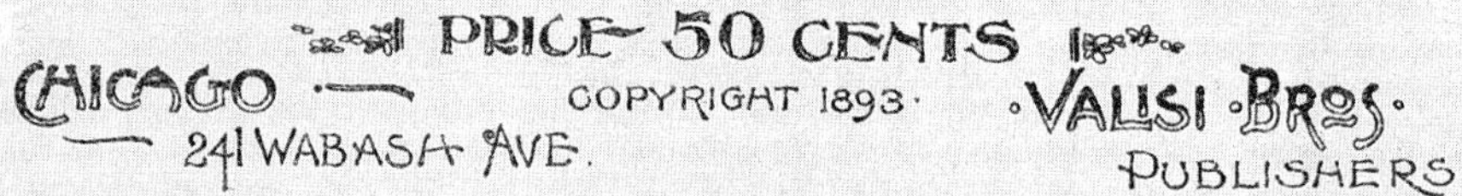

Special Morning Issue of the *Inter Ocean* on Chicago Day (Original size, 23½ by 18¼ inches)

The Chicago Day Poster (Original size, 32½ by 22 inches) [Chicago Historical Society]

CHICAGO DAY

at the

World's Columbian Exposition: Illustrated With Candid Photographs

G. L. Dybwad and Joy V. Bliss

Folding Map

Notes by:

Ruth Owen Jones
and
Thomas Yanul

The Book Stops Here
Albuquerque, New Mexico

1997

Other books by Dybwad and Bliss:

Annotated Bibliography: World's Columbian Exposition, Chicago 1893
James A. Michener, The Beginning Teacher and His Textbooks

Dybwad, G. L., and Joy V. Bliss
Chicago Day at the World's Columbian Exposition: Illustrated With Candid Photographs.

Includes index and bibliography.
1. World's Columbian Exposition, 1893
2. Photography
3. Chicago

ISBN: 0-9631612-3-7
Library of Congress Catalog Card Number: 97-92955

For information: The Book Stops Here, Publisher
1108 Rocky Point Court N.E.
Albuquerque, NM, 87123-1952
Telephone and Fax: (505) 296-9047
e-mail to: gldjvb@tarrnet.com

FIRST EDITION

Front cover illustration: *Official Souvenir Programme* cover (original size, 10 5/8 by 6 7/8 inches).
Back cover illustrations: Adult and child's tickets for Chicago Day (actual sizes).
Advertising souvenir: Facsimile of the final payment check for the World's Columbian Exposition written on Chicago Day (original size, 3 5/8 by 8 1/4 inches).

Printed in the United States of America.

TABLE OF CONTENTS

Dedicated to the Memory of our Fathers

Philip A. Dybwad 1917–1968

Harald N. Bliss 1911–1992

ACKNOWLEDGEMENTS

The authors thank Jim Emple for providing a photocopy of his souvenir Chicago Day program, including its color front cover. Ruth Owen Jones and Thomas Yanul contributed helpful conversations, as well as their written essays. Todd Gustavson of the George Eastman House, Rochester, New York, kindly gave us information about the Kodak No. 4 camera, its lens, and how the film could have been developed. He provided a complimentary copy of a relevant *Image* magazine.

We obtained experienced insights into the probable print process used for the candid photographs from Mo Palmer, Photography Archivist for the Albuquerque Museum, in Albuquerque, New Mexico; Richard Rudisill, Photographic Curator, and Arthur Olivas, Photographic Archivist, both from the New Mexico Museum in Santa Fe, New Mexico. Their experience, help, and suggestions were invaluable. We are thankful to the Chicago Historical Society staff for searching their files for a professional photographer with the initials "H. R. P. 2d"; no match was found.

We are grateful to Robert and Marjie Fania, formerly of St. Louis, Missouri, for informing us of the long-standing rivalry between St. Louis and Chicago. We appreciate the summary of that rivalry, which started long before the float fiasco at the Columbian Exposition, that we obtained from the Mercantile Library, St. Louis.

A hearty thank you to our neighbor and long-time Chicago resident, Howard Bouton, for Chicago information, helping us identify the train depots in that city, and proofreading the sections on transportation.

We are indebted to Peggy Sinko, Chicago researcher, for enthusiastic and professional participation in this project and to the Chicago Public Library for the interlibrary loan of their *Chicago Daily News* and *Chicago Herald* microfilm reels. We thank all our proofreaders and especially our final editors who were diligent beyond measure: Kathryn Lindell and Charlotte Norwood.

Charles E. Kirtley of Kirtley Auctions, Elizabeth City, North Carolina, kindly provided us with an image of the Chicago Day ribbon souvenir. James A. Vanek, Portland, Oregon, was very helpful in sending illustrations of the Chicago Day medal and philatelic cover. All three items are illustrated on page 16.

INTRODUCTION

Our bibliography on the World's Columbian Exposition held in Chicago, Illinois, in 1892–93 brought us into touch with publications by and about influential people at the fair, problems at the fair, the grand array of buildings, and international events associated with this watershed of United States history. The Columbian Exposition, which celebrated the four-hundredth anniversary of Christopher Columbus's landing on the Americas, generated an explosion of printed matter and many firsts such as the first picture postcards, the largest building in the world, World's Congresses on numerous subjects, and a grand opportunity for the growing rank of amateur photographers.

A chance find of a batch of mounted photographs from Chicago Day, October 9, 1893, at the fair quickly convinced us that describing that joyous day would not only capture the exuberant mood of the fair but also could be of value to those interested in early photography or in operating huge events smoothly. Putting the story together, we learned how photography became economically available to many but still required skill and some financial resources, as well as how the Chicago Day managers adeptly handled ticket sales, crowd control, security, concessions, transportation, entertainment, and publicity to create a memorable gathering.

Chicago Day is an example of the best in enjoyable American festivals and is a historical lesson that finds relevance today in theme parks, carnival midways, and even rock concerts.

Front Cover of the Bibliography Showing the Statue of the Republic by Daniel Chester French (original size, 11 by 8½ inches)

CHICAGO DAY. **The Chicago Daily Tribune.** FAIR WEATHER IS PREDICTED FOR TODAY.

VOLUME LII.—NO. 282. MONDAY, OCTOBER 9, 1893—TWENTY-FOUR PAGES.—WITH ART SUPPLEMENT. PRICE TWO CENTS.

OFFICIAL CHICAGO-DAY PROGRAM.

COMMITTEE ON WORLD'S FAIR.

WILLIAM R. KERR, Chairman.

JAMES L. FRANCIS, CHAS. SCHUMACHER, ALBERT H. KLEINECKE, JOHN O'NEILL, JOHN F. KENNY, CYRUS H. HOWELL, JAMES L. CAMPBELL, WILLIAM I. KENT, JOHN McGILLEN, EDWARD MARRENNER, JOHN W. HEPBURN, AUSTIN O. SEXTON.

The plan adopted by the Special Committee includes: I. A Welcome to the World in Music and Song, in the morning 10 to 12. II. A Reunion of States, illustrated by youths and maidens, at 2 p. m., and a Night Pageant. III. "Chicago in Her Growth Welcoming the World," to conclude with a Magnificent Display of Fireworks, and a Special Illumination of the Wooded Island and Midway Plaisance. The grounds and all the State Buildings open until midnight.

Chicago Hussars enter Midway Plaisance at 10 o'clock and make a tour of the grounds.

For the morning, 10 to 12 a. m.—Cannon "Salute to All Nations," Battery D, Lieut. F. Russell commanding. Chicago Welcomes the World in Music and Song. Apollo Club Chorus of 1,000 and Bands.

I. Fanfare of Universal Peace.—Four to eight Trumpeters in appropriate (herald's) uniform, to be stationed on the Columbian Arch Peristyle, the same on the Administration Building, and the same on the Manufactures and Liberal Arts, and opposite, thus flanking the Lagoon. These to play separately a short fanfare of peace, then altogether in unison so that the entire multitude may hear. Motto: "Peace on Earth, Good Will to Men." Trumpeters from Fort Sheridan by the courtesy of Gen. Nelson A. Miles.

II. Overture, "All Nations," by the combined bands.

III. "The Star Spangled Banner," by chorus of 2,000; the refrain sung by the multitude, each person waving a small hand flag in time with the music.

IV. Music of the Southern States. "Dixie Land," "Maryland," "Kentucky Home," etc. United Bands.

V. "Columbia, The Gem of the Ocean," Chorus, Orchestra, and Bands.

VI. Grand March. United Bands. Ringing of the Liberty Bell at noon by the Hon. Carter H. Harrison, Mayor of Chicago.

VII. "America" and Doxology by the multitude, with salute of cannon, bands at noon.

The program to be sung on terminal plaza on Chicago day at 11 o'clock a. m. will be rendered by 800 voices. Choral Director Tomlins will lead, and the songs will be of an international nature. It will consist of the following selections: "Die Wacht am Rhine," "Marseillaise," "Austrian Hymn," "Russian Hymn," "Keller's American Hymn," "Star Spangled Banner," "To Thee, My Country," "America," "Home, Sweet Home," "Suwanee River," selections by Liesegang's Band. Some of these will be repeated in Festival Hall at 4 o'clock p. m., with "part songs" and additional choruses.

Exhibition Drill in Stock Pavilion at 11 by Chicago Hussars, Capt. E. L. Brand commanding.

Program of Afternoon Spectacle and Procession—Reunion of the States at 2 o'clock p. m. at the Court of Honor. Review of States represented by youths and maidens, as follows:

First Section—Chorus of 100 boys from the Diocesan Choir, Mr. F. A. Dunster, Director. Chicago as a Guard of Honor, comprised of youths representing thirty-four wards, bearing shields with coat of arms and the word "Welcome." Sixth Presbyterian Cadets, Mr. H. F. Wenk, Drill Master. The thirteen original States, represented by young misses bearing State shields, olive branches, and wearing a crown with a star. Company of twenty-four boys in Continental uniform, selected from First Regiment Illinois Cadets, Mr. Place, Drill Master. Then follow all the States of the Union, the counties and principal cities represented in the following order: Standard with State shield, name of State and year of entry into the Union, borne by a standard bearer with two supporters. Six principal cities of each State, represented by maidens bearing pennants, various colors, with names of cities, or shields. Counties—First row of each group bearing some State emblem, such as sheaf of wheat, golden rod, etc., the others carrying a small flag. The procession of States aside from the original thirteen will be divided into four sections, as follows:

SECOND SECTION.

Will consist of the following States, represented by children from the following schools: Fuller, Doolittle, Oakland, Fifty-fourth Street, and Kenwood Schools.

State		Admitted		No. Counties
Vermont	admitted	1791.	No. Counties	14
Kentucky	"	1792.	"	119
Tennessee	"	1796.	"	96
Ohio	"	1802.	"	[illegible]
Louisiana	"	1812.	"	[illegible]
Indiana	"	1816.	"	[illegible]
Mississippi	"	1819.	"	[illegible]

Committee—B. F. Hill, Chairman; Miss Leona Thorne, A. L. Stevenson, Miss L. J. Price, Miss Sollitt.

THIRD SECTION.

Represented by children from the following schools: Brownell, Carter, Champlain, and Lewis.

State		Admitted		No. Counties
Illinois	admitted	1818.	No. Counties	102
Alabama	"	1819.	"	70
Maine	"	1820.	"	16
Missouri	"	1821.	"	115
Arkansas	"	1836.	"	75
Michigan	"	1837.	"	85
Florida	"	1845.	"	55

Committee—F. R. Ormsby, Chairman; Miss Abby Lane, Miss Nellie Gray.

FOURTH SECTION.

Will consist of the following States, represented by children from the following schools: Woodlawn, Moseley, Calumet, and Haven.

State		Admitted		No. Counties
Texas	admitted	1845.	No. Counties	212
Iowa	"	1846.	"	99
Wisconsin	"	1848.	"	[illegible]
California	"	1850.	"	54
Minnesota	"	1858.	"	80
Oregon	"	1859.	"	31

Committee—Miss Burke, Chairman; Mr. Spoon, Miss Dewy, and Mr. Bannon.

FIFTH SECTION.

Represented by the following schools: Duncan Avenue, Madison Avenue, Parkside, Brookdale, and Cornell.

State		Admitted		No. Counties
Kansas	admitted	1861.	No. Counties	102
W. Virginia	"	1863.	"	54
Nevada	"	1864.	"	14
Nebraska	"	1867.	"	[illegible]
Colorado	"	1876.	"	[illegible]
Washington	"	[illegible]	"	[illegible]
Montana	"	[illegible]	"	[illegible]
N. Dakota	"	[illegible]	"	[illegible]
S. Dakota	"	[illegible]	"	[illegible]

Committee—Miss Julia P. McEnhroe, Chairman; Misses Irene Fort, Johnson, Hinley, Kittie M. Howison, and Mrs. Joselyn and Mrs. Colt.

ORDER OF THE NIGHT PAGEANT.

Chicago in her growth receiving all Civilized Nations of the Earth. Chicago Hussars, Capt. E. L. Brand commanding, as escort. Band.

First Float—The Genius of Music. Surrounded by a Select Chorus of fifty ladies under Prof. G. Katzenberger's direction.

Second Float—Chicago, "I WILL." Guided by Love and Liberty and surrounded by all the States of the Union welcoming all peoples of the Globe; at the four corners, Music, Sculpture, Science, Literature. Chicago, Miss Flynn; Love, Miss Floy Strong; Liberty, Miss S. Cruver; Music, Miss Esther Gritzner; Art, Miss Caddie Mathews; Science, Miss Blanche Smithson; Literature, Miss Gertie Owen. Drawn by eight horses.

Third Float—Chicago in 1812—A Trading Post—Massacre! This float bears upon a high platform a group representing the famous Black Partridge in the act of rescuing a white woman from the savage Pottawatomie's tomahawk. Upon the sides of this raised central portion pictures are drawn representing the old Fort Dearborn and Mr. Kinzie's house. A glimpse of the ancient block house is shown on the front end, while immediately in advance an incident of the Indians' friendliness in rescuing a wounded officer is shown. Episodes of the Massacre are shown at the sides (the shooting of Capt. Wells), while at the rear a wigwam with a picturesque group of Indian traders, and a priest as well as singing maidens, give a peaceful aspect in pleasing contrast to the more sanguinary scenes. Rich skins, beads, and implements of war are used to ornament the corners. This float will be furnished with native American Indians of historical prominence, including the Pottawatomie Chief Simon Pokagon, whose father formerly owned the land upon which Chicago now stands. Three Cherokee maidens, Misses Rosa, Rena, and Carrie Bluejacket, will form a graceful group and sing an Indian song, which will form a most unique and authentic historical display. This float is in charge of Miss Emma C. Sickles, assisted by the following committee: William Penn Nixon, Maj. James Kirkland, Capt. Eli Huggins, Mr. Fred B. Tuttle (Calumet club), Mrs. Judge Trumbull, Mrs. Charles Wheeler, Mrs. Charles A. Sawyer. Drawn by six horses.

Fourth Float—Chicago in War. Sheridan's famous charge at the front. The figures of Grant and Logan, Douglas and Richard Yates (the "War Governor"), and finally Lincoln, with Chicago in the attitude of offering her sons. On the sides of the shipshape structure the dogs of war are being loosened by the Furies, while the mouths of cannon protrude in a suggestive manner. A most picturesque group, full of action and grace, closes the picture at the rear with a group of Ellsworth Zouaves, their famous Captain in the act of leading them in a charge. This group will be taken by some of the surviving veterans who served with honor and distinction under the gallant Ellsworth. Flags form the draperies, while the names of many of the heroes who fought and bled for the honor of the flag—the glory of the Garden City—will appear in the panels at the bottom of the float, among them Col. Mulligan, Capt. Barker, and Gen. Shields. The leading characters will be furnished by members of the Sheridan club.

Fifth Float—Chicago in Peace. This graceful float represents the Angel of Peace in a car drawn by a large number of Cupids, with trumpets, decorated with flowers. At the base, seated at the ends and sides, are four figures, typical of the Industries—Building, Textile Fabrics, Iron Manufactures, and Agriculture. The Cupids are modeled, the others are living figures. The sides are adorned with paintings of elevators and shipping scenes on the river and Lake Front. This will be drawn by six white horses.

Sixth Float—Chicago Prostrate (1871)—"The Fire Fiend." The great conflagration is typified by ruined fragments, columns, etc. A colossal figure, the "Fire Fiend," with devastating torch in hand, is being ineffectually opposed by some firemen ascending the steps; a mother is striving to protect her children and firemen are in the act of rescuing little ones. At the rear part a vision is seen of Chicago rising from its ashes, and a bricklayer is busy with mortar, etc. This float will be manned by the Chicago Fire Department, who will furnish the six horses as well.

Seventh Float—Commerce. This exquisite design represents an argosy with the single sail, on which the word "Commerce" is emblazoned, while the mast is decorated with festoons of flowers and evergreens. The figure of Commerce is seated upon the car, which is supported upon two iron wheels like those of a locomotive, and in front are the Three Graces offering their gift of flowers. At the sides are enormous cornucopias, or horns of plenty, with various fruits, while at the extreme rear the figure "Fortuna," upon a very high seat, adorned with wings at the base, may be seen guiding the boat. The surface represents water, in which the boat is sailing, and the extreme corners are decorated with female figures representing the various articles of agriculture, fruits, cereals, etc. This float will be in gold and white entirely, and drawn by eighteen horses, three abreast. It is the intention of the Board of Trade to have the heads of the horses decorated with electric lights—red, white, and blue. The sides of the vessel will also be a blaze of light from electricity, which will be furnished from batteries stored underneath. The horses will be led by men in the costume of the medieval ages, and the whole will form one of the most beautiful as well as significant features of the pageant, reflecting great credit upon all concerned.

Eighth Float—Columbus at the Court of Isabella. Columbus at the Court of Isabella will be the most magnificent and expensive float in the entire procession, illustrating as it does that moment of supreme dramatic interest when Isabella decides to offer up her jewels to furnish the means for the discovery of the Western World. A magnificent canopy of purple silk, lined with satin, supported upon four standards, is erected, underneath which may be seen the figures of Isabella and Ferdinand in the act of rising from their throne, while Columbus kneels to receive their blessing. Attendant ladies of the court are near, while the powerful Cardinal Talavera stands near by. Father Juan Perez is turning from the secretary and a group of monks in the attitude of thankfulness toward Isabella; while still further to the front are seen still a group of priests standing about a globe and discussing the project. The body of the float is constructed of solid wood, in the ecclesiastical style of architecture; with the exception of the center the entire float is encircled by an ornamental railing. At the front is the coat of arms of Castile and Aragon, standards with pennants flying from masts which are placed at the corners ornamented with Gorgons' heads. The whole float is furnished with rich rugs and tapestries from the Orient, and forms in itself a most gorgeous spectacle. The characters of the float will be taken and the costumes furnished by the Columbus club of this city. It will be drawn by six black horses.

The following Floats were furnished by foreign-born residents of Chicago, illustrating historic characters and great events.

Great Britain—The Early Discoveries and First Settlers. George E. Gooch, Chairman of the committee. This is in the form of a boat and represents, about the single mast in the center upon a raised platform, the Cabots with a globe. At the front stand Sir Walter Raleigh, Sir Francis Drake, and others. Nearer the center a group of Puritans, including Miles Standish and Priscilla. At the rear a group representing Capt. John Smith and Pocahontas. These historical characters will be taken by members of St. Andrew's, St. George's, and other societies of Englishmen in Chicago. The float will be drawn by twelve horses.

Sweden—Will be represented by the ancient legend, "The Vikings and Valkyries in Walhalla." G. L. Svenson and Robert Lindblom, committee. This float will be one of the most picturesque and gorgeous in the parade. The float will be drawn by twelve horses. On each will be a lady in the costume of the Valkyrie, and each animal will be led by a man dressed in a second century Viking costume.

Germany—Mr. Washington Hesing, Chairman of committee; Mr. Max Stern, Secretary. Two Floats, illustrating Germany in Art, Science, and Industry. Triumphal Arch in center, Germania standing on top of it; in the arch Guttenberg and Faust making the first press proof; Kepler, using the telescope; Bach, Kant, Liebig, Humboldt, Goethe, Schiller; a blacksmith; Electricity, represented by a lofty figure, bearing wings; Six Muses: Science, Drama, Music, Sculpture, Painting, Female Industry. The German-Americans in the History of the United States, 1776 and 1861—Center figure, Goddess of Liberty; German-American Generals, Muehlenberg, Steuben, De Kalb, Von Herkheimer, Sigel; Pennsylvania, German Soldiers at Valley Forge; Turner Company and Soldiers in Civil War (1861). Manned by the Chicago Turn-Gemeinde.

Ireland—Committee, Thomas Brennan, William J. English. Two Floats. St. Brendan, the first discoverer. The ancient Saint, in a boat with his followers, is being tossed upon the waves of the ocean. The Genius of Erin, surrounded by prominent Irish characters.

Bohemia—Joseph Hladovec, Chairman of committee. One Float—John Huss and his reformation; Freedom achieved by the people, and Bohemian industries preceded and followed by historical pageant in costume. The Bohemian allegorical float shows Art, Science, Industry, and Agriculture paying homage to Bohemia.

French Canadians—Committee, Joseph Beaugeau and Jacques Cartier club. Two Floats. "La Grande Hermine." This represents the first boat that bore the white men to the shores of Canada in 1534. The name of the boat was "La Grande Hermine," and the explorer, Jacques Cartier, with an Indian companion and boatman, is shown in the boat. Marquette landing in Chicago, 1673.

Denmark—H. S. Hagerup, Chairman of committee. Norway—F. A. Kean, Chairman of committee. Two Floats. Norway 1,000 years ago. Lief Erickson, the first discoverer of America. Norway at present. Columbia and Nora, or the Red, White and Blue of the Two Hemispheres. One Float—Dania.

Poland—Committee, C. J. Belinski, Frank Sowadski, Casimir Zychlinski. Four Floats. Washington, Kosciusko, and Pulaski, surrounded by Liberty, Continental soldiers, cannon, etc. Sobieski, with the Polish Duke before Vienna and the Turks bowing in submission. This represents the rescue of Vienna and Christendom from the thraldom of Turkish rule. Adoption of the Constitution of Poland, A. D. 1791 (May 3), Stanislaus taking the oath, surrounded by the nobility of Poland. Copernicus and historical characters devoted to Art, Science, and Literature: Copernicus, scientist; Kochanowski, poet; Mickiewicz, poet; Kraszewski, poet; Matejko, poet; Chopin, musician.

Electra—The Genius of Electricity will be represented by an enormous dragon, the color of which will be changed at intervals from green to red; 2,000 incandescent lamps used in lighting it. Drawn by eight horses.

ROUTE OF THE NIGHT PAGEANT—The floats will enter the grounds at the Sixty-second street entrance. The procession will then pass north of Choral Hall and turn south, past the Transportation Building. The pageant will pass around the court west of the Administration Building, skirting the MacMonnies Fountain, and continuing east on the northern side of the Court of Honor, around the Manufactures Building, and west over the Lagoon; then north on the east side of Horticulture and Woman's Buildings, past the west front of the Illinois Building and Art Gallery annex, moving east past the State Buildings and north front of Art Gallery; north at the New York Building, west from the Maryland Building, past Washington and California, and west of Horticultural Hall to Sixty-second street.

GRAND DISPLAY OF FIREWORKS—The display of fireworks will exceed in magnitude any which has heretofore been given in the United States, if not in the world. The great special pieces on the Lake-Front will be as follows: Old Fort Dearborn, the Old City Hall, the Portrait of the First Mayor of Chicago—William B. Ogden; Chicago Welcoming the World; Old Glory, the National Banner, carried by Mr. Baldwin, the aeronaut, in a balloon into the heavens; Chicago Triumphant, being a production of Niagara Falls in golden fire along the peristyle. The largest piece of the evening will be entitled the "Burning of Chicago," and will cover an area of 14,000 square feet, and be produced in four scenes. The first will illustrate Mrs. O'Leary's cow; second, the kicking over of the lamp; the fire starting thence gives a realistic and correct view of the burning of the city, closing with the picture of Chicago in ruins. In addition to this, flights of bombs, cascades of rockets, and every known variety of the pyrotechnic art will fill out the evening program. Other features will be the special illumination of the Wooded Island and fireworks set off from the water surrounding it, including a number of set pieces; also fireworks in the Midway Plaisance.

ROUTE OF THE GRAND NIGHT DAY PAGEANT.

Special Morning Issue for Chicago Day, October 9, 1893

THE SETTING: THE WORLD'S COLUMBIAN EXPOSITION

The World's Columbian Exposition in Chicago, Illinois, an idea born in the late 1880s, celebrated the four-hundredth anniversary of explorer Christopher Columbus and his pioneering sailing adventures to the Americas. The United States Congressional committee studying the celebration saw it also as a chance to display the burgeoning economic and industrial strength of the United States, bring the best of the world together in one place, and promote trade at the same time. The Paris Exposition of 1889, with its commanding trademark, the Eiffel tower, would not only be emulated; but the plan was to surpass it in every statistic and department.

Chicago's "I Will"

The site of the fair was debated at length. New York City, St. Louis, Chicago, and Washington, D.C., garnered the most votes in Congress with Chicago the ultimate winner on the eighth vote; President Benjamin Harrison signed the proclamation on April 25, 1890. Chicago's business and government leaders had won the day with ready capital backing from its industrialists, good transportation, and efficient and enthusiastic organization and planning. Having lost the bid to host the fair, New Yorkers felt Chicago should be named "The Windy City" due to long-winded oratory and braggadocio used in securing the site of the world's fair. That moniker stuck.

Thus in 1890, Chicago had to get to work and build just as it had done in 1871 after a large part of the city burned to the ground. The fair was a symbol of that courage, energy, and determination. The city motto in 1893 was "I Will," and it is still used today. Colonel Kohlsatt of the newspaper *Inter Ocean* had devised the contest which created that city motto and symbol.

Thomas W. Palmer, President of the World's Columbian Commission

The World's Columbian Commission, directed by Thomas W. Palmer, worked with the World's Columbian Exposition Company in Chicago headed successively by Lyman J. Gage, William Thomas Baker, and finally Harlow Niles Higinbotham whose tenure included Chicago Day, October 9, 1893. A Joint Council of Administration smoothed differences in planning philosophy between the two organizations.

Chicago chose a site from several city proposals: north side near Lincoln Park, southwest at Washington Park, and undeveloped land on the Lake Michigan shore destined to be Jackson Park. Jackson Park was chosen for its shoreline access, availability of 689 acres, and rapidly growing south-side communities. It provided the largest world's fair site to that time. Nearby, the University of Chicago opened in 1892; and Pullman village operated as a model city and passenger railcar factory.

Harlow N. Higinbotham, President of the World's Columbian Exposition

The landscape architects for the fair, Frederick Law Olmsted, designer of Central Park in New York, and his young partner Harry Codman, developed the shore property bounded by Fifty-sixth Street on the north to Sixty-seventh Street on the south and stretching west to

Stony Island Avenue, which nearly borders the extensive rail lines heading into the city to Dearborn, Union, and other train stations. Hence, both land and water transportation to the fair could be easily provided; the system, designed to carry 130,000 patrons an hour, was adequate for every day except one—Chicago Day. The use of lagoons and basins, a uniform cornice height for all twelve of the major buildings, and generally a uniform white or light color to the buildings led to the landscape and architectural success of the Columbian Exposition, the impact of which is still written about today. The "White City" with the world's largest structure, the Manufactures and Liberal Arts Building (see center building of illustration on page 3), was not only a monumental place to exhibit the products of mankind but also was a pleasing one to the eye and spirit.

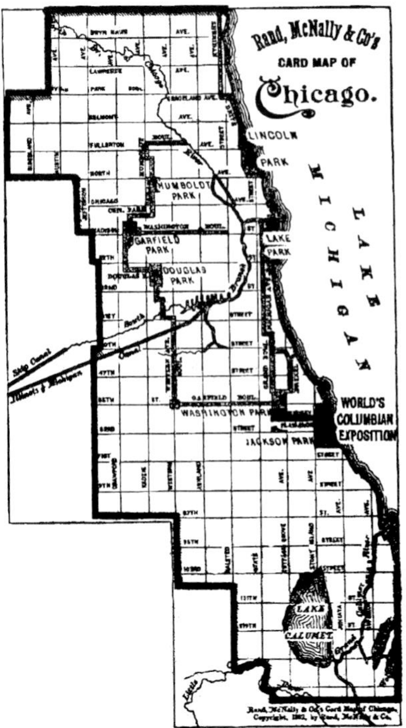

Chicago and the Site of the Exposition

Daniel Hudson Burnham

George R. Davis

Director of Works (Chief of Construction), Daniel Hudson Burnham, under Director-General George R. Davis, laid out the state and foreign buildings at the north end of Jackson Park and the main buildings around waterways that were dredged from shore bogs and which meandered through the grounds offering many enchanting views. The Agriculture Building and the Stock Pavilion were on the south end of the grounds and the Transportation and Terminal Station Buildings were fittingly located on the west side with easy spur access to main lines, not only to facilitate the two-year construction phase and the dedication in October 1892, but also to make entry into the fair attractive, easy, and inexpensive. The grand and imposing Administration Building, designed by Richard M. Hunt of New York, greeted fairgoers coming out of Terminal Station and overlooked the Court of Honor's basin and the huge gilt Statue of the Republic sculpted by Daniel Chester French, the whole serving as a focal point for the entire grounds.

Administration Building

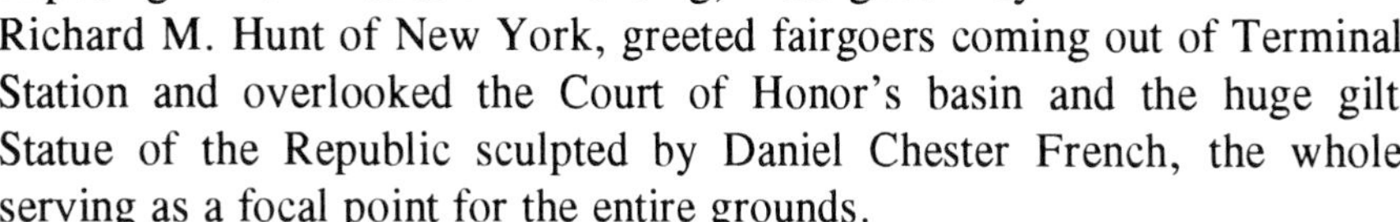

A distinctive feature of the grounds was the first-ever-dedicated Woman's Building, designed by Sophia G. Hayden. The promotion of this building, as well as the neighboring Children's Building and two dormitory buildings off the grounds for women and family visitors, by the Board of Lady Managers led to many accolades then as well as positive reviews which are still issued today. The Board was chaired by the indefatigable Chicago socialite Bertha (Mrs. Potter) Honoré Palmer. The removal of suffragette Phoebe Couzins from the Board for

Bertha Palmer

inappropriate management of funds did little to dampen the enthusiasm and extensive contributions of women at the fair.

Fine Arts Palace

Near the Woman's Building stood the largest state building, Illinois. The only building intended to be permanent was just to the north, the Fine Arts Palace designed by C. B. Atwood of Chicago. Most of the buildings were constructed of iron beams, wood, glass, and lathe; and the larger ones were coated with inexpensive "staff," a kind of temporary stucco made of hemp fiber, plaster-of-Paris, cement, and water, which was then quickly painted with the pneumatic spray gun invented at the fair during construction. Frank D. Millet, noted artist, was Chief of Decoration for the buildings. In the case of Fine Arts, ultimate safety from fire and other damage was required to attract the best works for display from around the world. Hence, unlike the other buildings, brick, mortar, and marble were used in its construction. After the fair, this building became the Columbian (Field) Museum, housing for display many of the exhibits shown at the world's fair. In 1937 the Field Museum, renamed for benefactor and department store mogul Marshall Field, moved north to its present site on Lake Shore Drive; and the original Fine Arts Building became the home of the Museum of Science and Industry. Continuing value from the fair and the fairgrounds after the celebration was part of the original plans for south Chicago.

Chinese Theater and Joss House

The first amusement midway originated at the World's Columbian Exposition. The Midway Plaisance, a strip of land south of Fifty-ninth Street, 600 feet wide and just short of a mile long, was connected to the west end of the main grounds near the Woman's Building. Originally designed by Frederic Ward Putnam as a living ethnology exhibit, promoter Sol Bloom took over the Midway and ran it as a show ground for amusement, relaxation, diverse foods, entertainment, and knowledge. Unlike the exhibits on the main grounds, many of the exhibits on the Midway required an entrance fee; and many concessions sold arts, crafts, and souvenirs. Exhibits ranged from learned, such as Zoopraxographical Hall where Eadweard Muybridge showed his moving horse and dog images and the Working Man's Home, to commercial, such as the Libbey Glass works, the Ostrich farm from California, and Hagenbeck's Zoological Arena for trained animals. Ethnology concessions covered living exhibits of Esquimaux from Labrador, Egyptians in the Street in Cairo, Dahomey natives from West Africa, Javanese, the Chinese Theater, and the popular Viennese, Irish, and German Village pavilions. Many exhibitors lived on the Midway. Amusements included the Ice Railway ride and the captive hydrogen-filled balloon ride, described later. Today we would say there was something for everyone.

Ferris Wheel on the Midway

The most famous ride was developed by engineer George W. G. Ferris—a 265-foot-high revolving wheel. Originally greeted with skepticism as too wild, unsafe, and expensive

(50 cents a ride), it quickly became a hit, making excellent return to its investors. The huge wheel, intended by fair managers as a symbol to rival the Eiffel tower, carried 2160 passengers at a time in a series of streetcar-sized enclosures. The view of the fairgrounds and city at the top was breathtaking. Indeed, a Ferris wheel is a common and popular attraction on today's midways and in touring carnivals. After the Columbian Exposition, the wheel was moved north to the amusement park near Lincoln Park and then to St. Louis for the 1904 world's fair; after that fair, it was demolished by a wrecking crew. Archaeologists now hunt its remnants in St. Louis. The lure and romance of that first great thrill-ride live on. Chicago's Midway Plaisance is still called that today, even though the attractions and barkers are gone; and the land has been returned to a wide strip of grass used by University of Chicago students for play, rest, and study. The Midway in 1893 would not hold all the shows and vendors who wanted to be at the fair; snack and souvenir shops lined the west side of Stony Island Avenue, and the Model Sunday School Building was located there also. Buffalo Bill Cody held his immensely popular Congress of Rough Riders "Wild West" show a block from the main grounds. The popularity of the fair and the midway later spawned the "White City" amusement park in south Chicago, which was modeled after the beaux-arts architectural theme of the original.

Model Sunday School

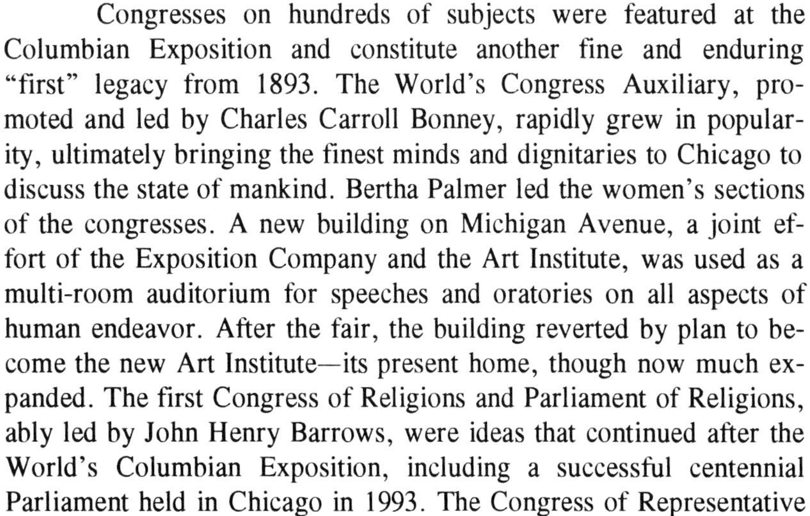

Congresses on hundreds of subjects were featured at the Columbian Exposition and constitute another fine and enduring "first" legacy from 1893. The World's Congress Auxiliary, promoted and led by Charles Carroll Bonney, rapidly grew in popularity, ultimately bringing the finest minds and dignitaries to Chicago to discuss the state of mankind. Bertha Palmer led the women's sections of the congresses. A new building on Michigan Avenue, a joint effort of the Exposition Company and the Art Institute, was used as a multi-room auditorium for speeches and oratories on all aspects of human endeavor. After the fair, the building reverted by plan to become the new Art Institute—its present home, though now much expanded. The first Congress of Religions and Parliament of Religions, ably led by John Henry Barrows, were ideas that continued after the World's Columbian Exposition, including a successful centennial Parliament held in Chicago in 1993. The Congress of Representative Women was held at the Art Institute, and the Congress of Women was held at the Woman's Building on the fairgrounds. This concept of airing achievements and needs in a central forum was an early realization of the growing interdependence and diversity of people on a small and fragile planet.

Charles C. Bonney

This fair, held from May 1 to October 30, 1893, was an important part of "the gay '90s." It evolved into a historical event because of the people who supported it, the wealth of information disseminated, clever promotion, enduring symbols, glittering architecture, and the ideal park-like

The Art Institute on Michigan Avenue

setting. The overall success in all departments, including financial, was tempered by some disasters and failures. Impressionist painters, considered too radical, were not exhibited. The Cold Storage Building with its efficient but dangerous ammonia cooling plant burned to the ground on July 10, costing lives and, temporarily, the peace of mind of fair attendees. The grounds were at times closed on Sunday to observe the Sabbath; when they were opened, after pleas from working men and children to experience this educational opportunity and requests from exhibitors trying to pay their costs, many exhibits were closed, and facilities—such as piped-in Hygeia water—were not available. Carter H. Harrison, popular four-term mayor, was assassinated on October 28, 1893, after spending a day at the fair just two days before it closed. The ultimate disaster was the financial panic of 1893–94 which caused bankruptcy for many, labor unrest, and strikes. Several fires in early 1894 destroyed large portions of the once proud and beautiful, but closed, World's Columbian Exposition; many exhibits had already been removed; but many were lost; and anticipated revenue from salvage operations went to zero in a few hours time. The idealism exemplified by the fair gave way to the need to improve the lot of many groups. Entrepreneur George M. Pullman feared for his life at the hands of distraught workers at his model railcar assembly plant; President of the national commission, Thomas W. Palmer, had a nervous breakdown due to the constant attention the Exposition required.

In spite of setbacks and criticisms, the overwhelming list of firsts at the fair, the financial and organizational successes, the large number of people who gained notoriety such as energetic prominent journalist Moses P. Handy, Head of Publicity and Promotion, and George W. G. Ferris, leave us with a feeling of awe, respect, and curiosity to know more about this grand microcosm of national and international life which contains lessons for us today.

Moses P. Handy

George W. G. Ferris

ADDITIONAL CHICAGO DAY SOUVENIRS NOT MENTIONED IN TEXT

Chicago Day Aluminum Medal Made by S. D. Childs & Co., Chicago. City Seal Obverse and "I Will" Motto Reverse (Actual Size)

Chicago Day Ribbon (Actual Size)
[Red, White, and Blue Button and Flag]

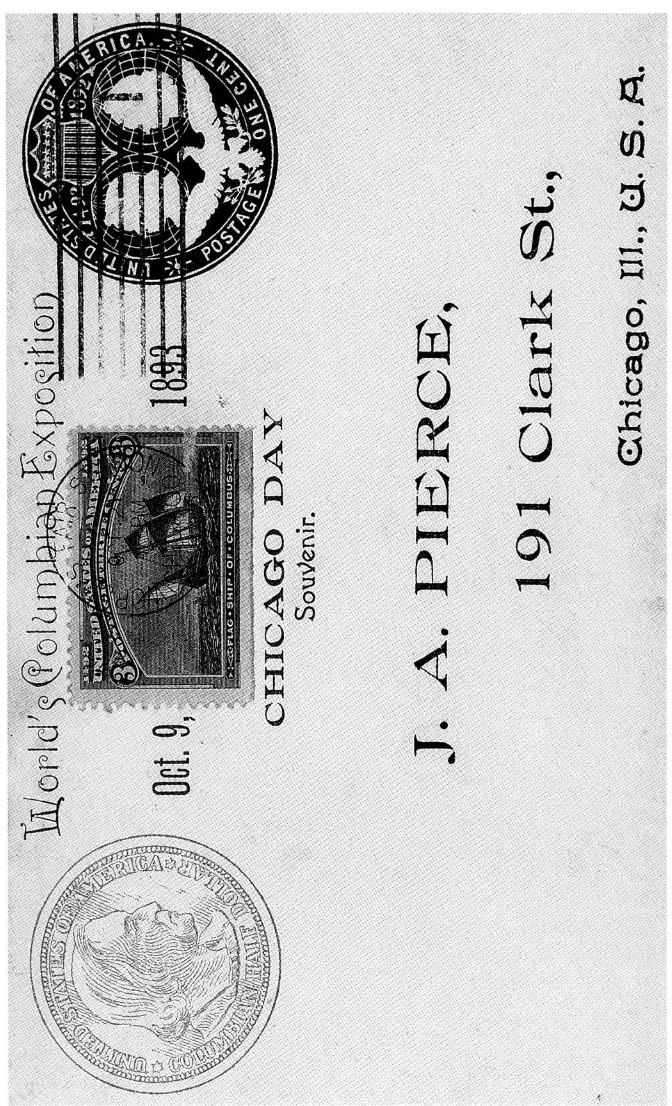

Chicago Day Envelope from Stamp Dealer, J. A. Pierce (Actual Size)
[Buff Envelope With Columbian Half-Dollar Cachet in Red. World's Fair Station Cancel on October 21, 1893, Over 3-Cent Columbus Commemorative]

PLANNING CHICAGO DAY

AUGUST 1893

What turned out to be the greatest day at the World's Columbian Exposition was not even mentioned until late in the six-month run of the fair. Rand, McNally's great guide, *A Week at the Fair*, and the detailed *Official Directory* issued by the Exposition, both published in early 1893, offer a list of fete days at the fair, but neither defined October 9 as Chicago Day.

On August 14, 1893, the *Chicago Tribune* carried a brief editorial comment mentioning "Chicago's day"—the earliest public mention we found. This was followed on August 18 by a half-column announcement on page three describing the event. The proposal that it be held on October 9 and entirely within the fairgrounds had been advanced by the city and agreed to by the Joint Council of Administration of the World's Columbian Exposition. Three basic features of the day were contained in the first proposal: (1) a march around the grounds by teenagers representing the states, counties, and major cities and a large chorus floating on a platform in the middle of the Basin; (2) a parade of floats at dusk illustrating Chicago history, intended to eclipse all other parades; and (3) a fireworks display costing $10,000 to include set pieces as large as 100 feet in length. Each of these was modified greatly and expanded over the course of the next seven weeks.

Alderman William R. Kerr

City alderman William R. Kerr had devised the idea for a city fete day. Born in 1849, his family moved to Chicago in 1868, just before the great fire. When he moved back to Chicago with his wife and three children, he had spent part of the intervening 20 years out of state in the insurance business. In 1891 he became a land developer and was instrumental in developing the successful Morgan tract west of Pullman, Illinois. It soon rivaled the Pullman housing and manufacturing center in south Chicago. Kerr was a Republican interested in bettering the city and became alderman from the thirty-second of Chicago's 34 wards. On a national level, he had been a delegate to the national convention supporting James G. Blaine, then Secretary of State, for the presidency. It was his suggestion that Mayor DeWitt C. Cregier appoint a citizens' committee of 100 to go to Washington, D.C., and urge the claims of Chicago for hosting the world's fair. Thus, he was an enthusiastic supporter of the Exposition and threw his whole energies into making Chicago Day a city celebration, as well as a national event. Kerr was named director of Chicago Day on August 22, 1893. His passion produced a wonderful festival.

Although the proposed event garnered only back-page-newspaper coverage for a month, its planners were clearly busy. They announced that it was not only going to be a 22-year "birthday" party celebrating Chicago's courageous rise from the ashes of the 1871 fire but also was intended to set a new paid-attendance record. Challenging the record had the clever effect of turning the fete day into a contest. After the fire, the city had used its big shoulders and grit to rebuild—and rebuilt with safety and permanence in mind. This Midwest crossroads for grain and livestock, accessible by water and rail, was not defeated. Architecture flourished; the disaster had been an opportunity to revitalize and plan anew. Architects such as William L. B. Jenney, Daniel H. Burnham, John Wellborn Root, Louis H. Sullivan, Frank Lloyd Wright, and others developed a new pattern of traffic and skyscraper construction in which the steel frame holds up the walls. The result was a changed city skyline. In 1893 the fiery waste laid by "Mrs. O'Leary's cow" was contrasted with a new Chicago and the structural magnificence and vistas of the White City, which Chicago had built for the enjoyment and benefit of the entire world. The city had an approximate population of 250,000 in 1871 which had grown to about 1,250,000 by 1893. Chicago Day would celebrate the city's renewal.

Brief articles demonstrated that local newspapers supported the plan for Chicago Day even though they were busy reporting the myriad daily events and activities at the fair; their support was essential for good publicity. Another key feature of the publicity campaign was designing, printing, and distributing an advertising poster just for October 9. The bold five-color poster (see page 4) approved at the end of August, shows the main elements of the planned festivities: a youth parade around the Court of Honor (rather than teenagers marching around the grounds), an evening pageant of allegorical floats, and a night illumination with electric lights and fireworks. In cooperation with the railroads, the city's planning committee had these broadsides put up in depots across the nation.

By the end of August, the plan expanded to include an opening ceremony to begin at 10 a.m. and musical programs to be held throughout the day. The fireworks set pieces were now anticipated to be as large as 200 feet in length.

SEPTEMBER 1893

The World's Columbian Commission for the Exposition, consisting of U.S. government appointees, endorsed Chicago Day in writing on September 1:

> *Resolved:* That the National Commission cordially indorses the program for Chicago day as outlined in the preliminary announcement and especially that feature relating to the reunion of States represented by youths and maidens from the cities and counties of the various States. Exalting as it does the spirit of national unity, this idea should receive the cordial support of every patriotic citizen, and this commission promises its hearty support and will do all in its power to assist in carrying it out.

The city committee gained the support of Mayor Carter H. Harrison in early September, including a plan for his Chicago Day proclamation that would make October 9 a city holiday. The *Tribune* reminded readers on September 14 that Chicago Day would, propitiously, fall on a Monday, making a long weekend; hence, there was no excuse from buying tickets and attending. The committee pressed the local railroads to reduce fares into Chicago so that all of Illinois would be induced to attend the celebration; the target rate was one cent a mile. The Alton road was the first to announce half fares for distances up to 300 miles from Chicago. Local newspapers carried longer and more positive editorials about Chicago Day, which appealed to everyone's patriotism. By mid-month, the city was prepared to field historical floats and called on local clubs to submit ideas and entries also. Papers printed attendance figures for past fete days so everyone would know the number of attendees needed to make Chicago Day a record for the Exposition.

Chicago, not the World's Columbian Exposition Company, planned Chicago Day. The first defined element, a "Reunion of States" parade around the Court of Honor, was fully organized on September 10. Kerr's "Committee on World's Fair" was comprised of 12 alderman of which O'Neill, Campbell, and Francis were the most active. They moved into special celebration headquarters in the Title and Trust building at 100 Washington Street, room 401, donated to them by businessman Thomas Cratty. The governor of Illinois, John P. Altgeld, made Chicago Day official by proclamation on September 21, 1893:

Committee on World's Fair	**William R. Kerr, Chairman**	
James L. Francis	Albert H. Kleinecke	John F. Kenny
James L. Campbell	John McGillen	John W. Hepburn
Charles Schumacher	John O'Neill	Cyrus H. Howell
William D. Kent	Edward Marrenner	Austin O. Sexton

> State of Illinois, Executive Office, Springfield, Ill., Sept. 21, 1893.—To the People of the State of Illinois: Monday, Oct. 9, next, will be the twenty-second anniversary of the day on which the great City of Chicago was burned to the ground. In the short time which has elapsed since that day the people of that city have not only rebuilt it on a scale of magnificence and grandeur

> which astonishes the world, but they have carried most of the burden and been the moving and directing force in creating that great White City by the lake [which] is attracting the nations of the earth to our gates. It has been decided to make Oct. 9 Chicago day at the World's Columbian Exposition and to hold the anniversary celebration there, and I hereby call upon all the people of the State who glory in its career and are proud of Chicago to do what in them lies to make this celebration a grand success and an occasion not to be forgotten.
>
> John P. Altgeld, Governor

Business Closures

On the same day businessmen in the city received a written memorandum from Kerr and the committee encouraging the October 9 closure of businesses and trades. It read in part:

> *Resolved.* That all clubs, the board of trade and stock exchange, the builders' and traders' exchange, the real estate board, the board of underwriters and all other organizations and businesses close on Monday October 9 in favor of Chicago Day.

Kerr announced his desire that saloons be closed as well—a proposal which had little effect. Large companies, such as Montgomery Ward, Chicago Brewing Company, and Fuller & Fuller Company, led the way, followed by myriads of smaller companies, each of which had its name printed in local papers.

Service-related facilities joined in the growing gala atmosphere. Postmaster Sexton wrote to Assistant Postmaster Jones in Washington, D.C., requesting permission to curtail mail deliveries so that workers could attend Chicago Day. He was successful: A single delivery would be made in the morning, and offices would close at 10 a.m.

Kerr went further by boldly suggesting that each company buy complimentary tickets to the fair for its employees. This caught on like a prairie wildfire, and soon giants like Marshall Field and Company, Mandel Brothers, Siegel Cooper & Company, and E. M. Knox, the hatter, were reserving large blocks of tickets.

Public and corporate acceptance of a city holiday at the fair was mounting.

Transportation

Of particular interest to promoters was cheap transportation. John Hepburn of the Committee On World's Fair was in charge. As mentioned, decreases in rates from local railroads were obtained first; and then reduction of rail rates were sought from all lines coming into Chicago. Again, the target was a penny a mile plus other incentives, about half the normal rate. An early goal of Chicago Day was to create a new first for the Exposition by breaking the all-time, one-day attendance record of about 397,000 visitors set at the 1889 Paris fair. Inexpensive and ample transportation was essential to meet this goal. The Eastern lines, such as the New York Central and Pennsylvania Railroads, were the first national lines to agree to the lower rates; the Western lines, such as the Atchison, Topeka & Santa Fe, joined in later. Low rates were available for one-way and round-trip fares. All roads were finding increased passenger usage as word of the stunning show in Chicago spread across the land. World's fair specials were run on most lines; normal routes frequently carried extra cars. Lowering rates for Chicago Day benefited both the railroads with increased passengers and the fair with increased attendance on subsequent days.

Reunion of States Children's Parade

The *Chicago Herald* carried a lengthy article on September 19 describing the novel and central feature for Chicago Day: thousands of school children would march in a parade entitled "Reunion of States." The children, admitted free, would wear colorful costumes and hats, carry banners, and flags representing Illinois cities and counties and all the other states and major cities. Flowers would abound. Boys and girls above the fourth grade would alternate in the ranks, and lead children would wear liberty caps and carry shields bearing the inscription "Welcome" or the name of the city and state they would represent. Thomas Brennan, chairman, issued cards for volunteers at every local school and spoke to parents about the planned spectacle scheduled for 2 p.m. on October 9. The idea was met with great enthusiasm, and more than enough students signed up. Fred A. Dunster would lead a processional band and the Diocesan Choir. All participants would form up behind the Peristyle (the colonnade east of the Basin), proceed around the Basin, and end at extensive seating that started near the Peristyle and stretched to the water's edge. No speeches were to be given, but the children would sing patriotic songs such as "Love and Liberty."

Ferdinand Peck

The very next day Ferdinand W. Peck, chairman of the Union League Club and First Vice President of the World's Columbian Exposition, announced a program to collect funds to pay for free tickets for other young attendees who could not afford the 25-cent entrance fee; more than $200 was subscribed the first day.

These activities to admit children free for Chicago Day illustrate that the fair was finally recognized as an educational opportunity.

Floats

Grand floats would provide an incentive to attend the celebration day too. No commercial floats would be allowed; but rather allegorical, patriotic, and technical floats were sought. The proud and active ethnic sections of Chicago—such as the Italians (John Garibaldi); Poles (John Kralovel); Irish (John F. Finerty); British (George E. Gooch); Norwegians (Lund C. Jevner); Swedes (Robert Lindblom); Swiss (Jacob Mans); Bohemians (J. Hladoveck); Holland (Consul George Birkhoff); Hungarian (Adolph Storm); and Germans (George A. Schmidt)—quickly formed committees under their leaders to respond by proposing floats, in some cases several from each group.

An early entry was the "Genius of Electricity" sponsored jointly by General Electric and the Chicago Edison Company. The dazzling float would be drawn by eight matched horses and have its own on-board boiler, engine, and dynamo powering over 2000 lamps exceeding 10,000 total candle power—then the common unit of luminosity. The 38-foot long by 9-foot wide by 28-foot high papier-mâché float in the shape of a dragon would use steam from the boiler to furnish alternately red and then green fiery breath issuing from the mouth of the monster. The theme would be the science of electricity and lighting overcoming darkness and ignorance, thus avoiding direct commercialism. This demonstration is a forerunner of such famous evening spectaculars as the Disney Main Street Parade.*

A city historical float "Fort Dearborn" featuring Pottawatomie Indians was announced. The evening lights around the grounds were to be extinguished as the floats entered so that the calcium chemical lights** on the floats could be best appreciated. A "Chicago Fire" float would be sponsored by the Builders' and Traders' Exchange. The galleries of the Transportation Building would serve as dressing rooms for costumed participants on the floats.

Not satisfied with local floats alone, Kerr sent committee members O'Neill, Campbell, and Francis on trips to Kansas City and St. Louis seeking to obtain floats from fraternal organizations—the Priests of Pallas and Veiled Prophets, respectively. Both cities were scheduled to hold parades just prior to Chicago Day, so floats would be available; and each city could potentially send many residents to Chicago for October 9. The case of the St. Louis floats was most demanding, since that city still harbored latent resentment towards Chicago for snatching the right to host the Exposition; but both organizations were quite receptive and offered early guarantees for floats and attendees. In turn, the

---

* Disney's parents went to the Columbian Exposition. Walt was born in Chicago in 1901 and most likely heard about the fair from them.

** Used in the theater and called limelight. A block of calcium oxide was heated white-hot by an oxygen and hydrogen flame to produce a brilliant illumination.

Chicago committee offered to pay rail charges and safe transit for the floats. Both of the city groups were capable of offering over 20 floats from which Chicago could choose the best and most fitting for the occasion. At this point, the committee expected a total of about 30 floats for the Night Pageant.

Tickets and Souvenirs

The Committee on World's Fair wisely recognized that a souvenir ticket for October 9 would help set the day apart from all others at the fair. The ticket design (illustrated on back cover) included a perforated stub that the patron could keep after entering the grounds. Kerr ordered 500,000 adult and 50,000 child's special tickets to be printed; they became available on September 30. Requests for the tickets came into committee headquarters continuously and were reported by the press with high anticipation: "These tickets are expected to sell like hot cakes." Kerr was quoted in an interview of September 29: "Our success thus far has been as satisfactory as we could expect it to be. There seems to be a general determination on the part of business houses and the public generally to make Chicago Day a memorable one in the history of the Exposition. Orders for the souvenir tickets are coming in by every mail." Edward Marrenner of the committee was in charge of ticket sales. Lowering the price of the 25-cent child's ticket became a subject of public debate.

In addition to keepsake tickets, a special badge was being designed to designate the important Chicago Day visitor, just as printed T-shirts today designate special visitors to events and places. The badge design had "Chicago Day" embossed on a pin-backed bar above a ribbon-draped Columbian silver half-dollar. (The implemented design is illustrated on page 1.)

The *Chicago Tribune* launched its own "souvenir" on September 16 by starting a game to guess the exact paid attendance for October 9. First- and second-place prizes would be $15 and $10 in gold, respectively—approximately a $300 and $200 value in today's gold market. The next 50 best guesses would gain free admission. Coupons, like the one reproduced, were printed in each weekday paper. Since originals had to be submitted, the paper's contest generated larger daily sales. To handle the flood of over 100,000 entries, a special tabulation room was established at the paper. Other local papers speculated as to the final paid attendance likely for Monday. Figures ranged from 300,000 to 700,000. Chicago Day had taken on the appealing guise of a contest with a world record and civic pride at stake.

TRIM TO THIS LINE.

The Chicago Tribune

Prize Guessing Contest

—FOR—

Chicago Day, Oct. 9, 1893.

I guess that the paid attendance (official) at the World's Columbian Exposition, Chicago Day, Oct. 9, 1893, will be ________

Name ________

Town ________

Street ________

Number ________

TRIM TO THIS LINE.

Contest Coupon from the *Tribune*

Fair Debt Closure

Kerr and his committee coordinated all their plans for Chicago Day with the officials. The Exposition Company was close to paying off its total debt, including the debenture bonds; and the committee on their behalf announced that the final payment would be made on October 9. This payment would greatly add to the festivities. The *Chicago Herald* promptly issued a scathing editorial on September 29 condemning the fair directors for deluding the public, building false confidence, and promoting Chicago Day.

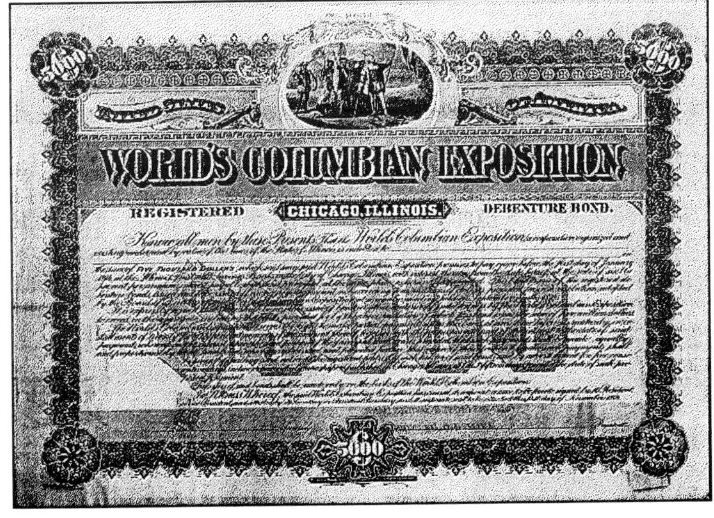

$5000 Columbian Exposition Debenture Bond

The *Herald* felt there was no way the bonds could be repaid at that time.

Thus, in about six weeks, with lofty goals, Chicago had laid out a bold framework for a city day at the fair and attempted to create for itself and the country a memorable historical moment worthy of a city that had rebuilt with style and flare after a devastating fire. Chicago Day news hit the front page of the *Tribune* for the first time on September 20 and did not retreat from there until October 12. This signified a growing enthusiasm for the project. Plan details were expanding exponentially on all fronts, and so was press coverage.

Not all of the plans and schemes, however, were successful. The city council passed a resolution inviting President Grover Cleveland, his wife, and new baby; and Ferdinand W. Peck of the Union League Club announced on September 14 that he intended to go to Washington, D.C., to present the proposal. The President, re-elected to a second—but not consecutive—term, respectfully declined by letter dated September 28, 1893, which was signed by his Private Secretary, Henry T. Thurber.

OCTOBER 1893

The Chicago Day committee put fresh plans before the public just eight days before the event. The local papers were quick to provide extensive details. This enthusiastic journalism did much to turn this local celebration into one that the whole country wanted to attend and witness.

Music

No extravaganza would be complete without music, so the organizers issued to the press an expanded list of musical events of all types to be available in various locations around Jackson Park.

It was planned that Lieutenant Alfred Russell from Chicago Battery D, U.S. Army, would fire a lakefront 21-gun salute at 10 a.m. Four groups of four heraldic-costumed trumpeters would then officially start the celebration of Chicago Day from the Court of Honor. Each quartet would present the thrilling fanfare from lofty quadrants: the top of Manufactures Building, Agriculture Building, Administration, and the Columbus Arch at the Peristyle; symbolically, these would represent the four great continents of the earth. Chicago's Fort Sheridan would provide the 16 musicians for this program feature, which was modified drastically several times before becoming finalized.

To follow until noon would be patriotic songs and national and international airs accompanied by 200 musicians and chorus of 2000 adults all situated in stands at the east side of the Administration Building. Visitors would be invited to add their voices to the more popular pieces. General Nelson A. Miles, Union Army hero and Indian fighter, was stationed in Chicago and commissioned Major G. W. Baird to write a verse for the inaugural chorus. Silas Gamaliel Pratt, Chicago Day program director, wrote the music.

S. G. Pratt

General Miles

William L. Tomlins, Music Director of the Exposition, announced the 11 a.m. program for his 800-voice chorus and Liesegang's Chicago Band, scheduled to take place west of the Administration Building. The Russian Choir led by Eugenie Lineff would perform in Festival Hall (Choral Building) at 11:30 a.m., and she advertised that all children would be admitted free to the concert.

The music and songs for the children's parade at 2 p.m. had already been announced and enthusiastically supported; more details about the 3000-person parade were now issued. The order of march was defined, practice was scheduled for 1 p.m. on Sunday in the Stock Pavilion, and assembly would take place at 1 p.m. Monday. Each child would be given a red and blue badge bearing a figure of the "I Will" maiden with the words "Chicago Day, World's Fair, Oct. 9, 1893."

Proud of Chicago, the Illinois Board of World's Fair Commissioners also made special plans for October 9. The Illinois Building would be emblazoned with bunting and flowers, and flags on cables would stream down from the top of its high dome to both ends of the building. A series of bands would play all day thus encouraging visitors to stop, enter the building, and see the bounty the state had to offer. Illinois Day had been held on August 24 with the second largest crowd to that date of 243,951 paid attendees.

Fireworks

The Independence Day pageant on July 4 at the fair, with its paid crowd of 283,273, had included a grand display of lights and fireworks. For Chicago Day, H. James Paine, the head of pyrotechnics at the world's fair, and his crew would have to exceed that effort by wide margins. The fireworks plan developed in August for October 9 paled compared with the grandiose plans issued in October. At least 50 additional experts from the New York factory had been added to handle all the sites and activities. Fireworks would be ignited from the lakefront, Lagoon, Court of Honor, Wooded Island, and Midway Plaisance. Special emphasis would be placed on huge mechanically animated "set pieces" lit by multicolored flares wired to frames and representing relevant themes such as "Burning of Chicago" (14,000 square feet) which would include Mrs. O'Leary's cow kicking over the lantern, "Old City Hall," "William Butler Ogden" (first mayor of Chicago), "Chicago Welcomes the World," "Old Fort Dearborn," "Falls of Niagara," "Chicago Triumphs," and others. "Old Glory" depicted by flares would be carried aloft above the grounds by balloonist Samuel Yates Baldwin. Wooded Island, in addition to being surrounded by aquatic fireworks, would itself be illuminated like a fairyland with 15,000 multicolor lamp flares. A finale of 5000 rockets and shells would go up from the lakefront.

Creative fireworks, held several times a week, was a hallmark of the fair and drew and kept many a spectator.

Speeches

Mayor Carter H. Harrison would proclaim the merits of Chicago and Chicago Day at noon and ring the New Liberty Bell, which was prominently hanging from a stout beam frame before the west entrance of the Administration Building. This Liberty Bell had been cast from melted pennies given by school children throughout the land as well as donated silver and other historical artifacts—not without attendant controversy. The shiny new replica, especially founded for the Exposition, was rung on many fete days at the fair but never so many times as it would ring on Chicago Day. The 3 p.m. and 5 p.m. pealing would be generated by ranking representatives of all the exhibited countries at the fair. To aid this process, a long, symbolic, clapper cord was fashioned using fibers or strands grown in each of the 42 countries exhibiting at the fair. Donated materials ranged from flax to fox fur.

The New Liberty Bell, West Entrance of Administration

Of special note would be a speech and poem written on white birch bark to be given by 70-year-old Simon Pokagon, Chief of the Pottawatomie Indians who had originally settled on the lakeshore. The speech, "The Red Man's Columbian Greeting," would lament the loss of native land and way of life but ask all to live in peace and harmony and use the Chicago site wisely. Then, in a special ceremony at 3 p.m., Pokagon would hand the 1833 deed for the Chicago land over to the city fathers and ring the

New Liberty Bell. Local papers were quick to point out that the Pottawatomie had still not been paid for the land, about three cents an acre. And, finally, Pokagon would be an honored guest on the "History of Chicago" float, chaired by Emma C. Sickles, Indian rights advocate.

Floats

The *Tribune* published a list of the proposed first 20 floats on October 1.

Float I	"Chicago" (receiving the nations)
Float II	"Chicago in 1812" (with Buffalo Bill and Cherokee singers)
Float III	"Chicago in War" (Sheridan Club depicting Grant's charge, Logan, Douglas, and Lincoln)
Float IV	"The Fire Fiend" (the Chicago conflagration including "Old Economy No. 8"* which saw service in 1871 and was still working)
Float V	"Chicago in Peace"
Float VI	"Chicago in Commerce"
Float VII	"Elestra" (the electric industries' steam-spouting electrical dragon)
Float VIII	"Columbus at the Court of Isabella"
Float IX	"Discoverers of Great Britain"
Floats X-XII	By the Swedish residents
Floats XIII, XIV	"Germany in Art and Science" and German residents
Floats XV, XVI	"Irish Discoverer St. Brandon" and "Genius of Erin"
Float XVII	Historic Bohemia
Float XVIII, XIX	Famous Poles and Polish history
Float XX	Denmark's Society Dania

At that point, all floats were presented by Chicago and its ethnic groups; Italy, whose fete day was October 12, was expected to provide some additional, as was Norway.

Almost daily, fresh details on the "final" array of floats were printed in the papers. Indeed, variations in the float parade occurred up until the wee hours of the special day itself. The volatility started when negotiations and arrangements for obtaining the volunteer floats from Kansas City and St. Louis failed. In the case of the Priests of Pallas from Kansas City, the Rock Island and Santa Fe lines refused to carry any of the floats because of their extreme width. The Veiled Prophets in St. Louis soundly snubbed Chicago aldermen O'Neill and Francis by emphatically withdrawing their floats on October 3. The Prophets felt the expense of modification of the floats to meet the needs of Chicago Day would be excessive; they were a social group not bound by the wishes of the city of St. Louis; and, furthermore, they felt their participation had not been invited in a proper manner. The *Sunday Tribune* cartooned the refusal on the front page of its October 8 edition. The rivalry between the two cities had started in the 1870s based on economics; it spread to baseball, the contest to hold the Exposition, and then, the Veiled Prophet floats.** Chicago was on its own.

***Tribune* Cartoon**

The Irish had their day on September 30 and were ready for Chicago Day, especially since a tiff had broken out among F. D. Millet, George R. Davis, Chief of the Electrical Department John P. Barrett, and the Irish committee on that special day. The Irish flag had been raised twice on a staff on the Electricity Building, only to be cut down, and finally removed to Millet's office across the way in the Administration Building. The abiding rule was that only nations recognizing the United States Navy flag—not the case for Ireland in 1893—could fly flags on Exposition poles. Daniel Burnham

---

* Called "No. 8" in the *Tribune* and "No. 9" in the *Herald.*

** The Veiled Prophets, originally founded as a harvest fair, currently hold their parade and fair around the Fourth of July at the Riverfront park area in St. Louis.

finally struck a compromise with Millet, and the Irish flag flew all day at the southern entrance arch of the Electricity Building. Swiss delegates, whose country's flag flew on prominent poles for the entire fair, chuckled at the spectacle produced by the Irish flag. The attendance on Irish day was 108,885.

The Sheridan Club in Chicago, named for Civil War Army hero General Philip Sheridan, would field the "Chicago in War" float. After the war, Sheridan was based in Chicago, commanding a large district; his troops kept order after the devastating city fire of 1871. The other honorees on the float would be Illinois native sons. One of them, Ulysses S. Grant, was selling hides with his brothers in Galena, Illinois, when the Civil War broke out. Later at Springfield, he trained troops for the North and was made a colonel due to his natural leadership ability.

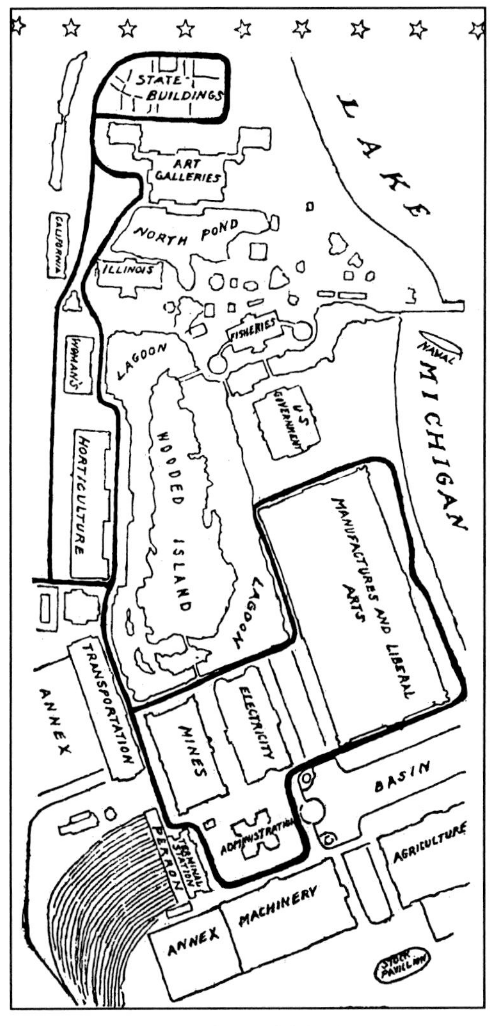

Parade Route for the Night Pageant

Miss Elizabeth A. Flynn would represent the "I Will" maiden on the lead float. Plans were for her to wear an electrically lit crown representing phoenix rising from the ashes, the headdress being attached to a hidden generator. Misses Florence L. Strong would symbolize "Love"; S. Cruver, "Liberty"; Ella Pierson, "Science"; Esther Gritzner, "Music"; Caddie Mathews, "Art"; and Emma Lindenberg, "Literature." They showed up at headquarters on October 6 to determine their costumes. The *Tribune* presented portrait cuts of the women on October 7. The parade was taking on a personal character, which the press followed avidly.

Each float in the Night Pageant would be preceded by a sign-bearer proclaiming the title of the presentation. Teams of eight to twelve matched and mounted horses would pull each float.

Norwegian residents announced intentions to enter two floats: "Norway 1000 Years Ago" and "Norway Now." Poland would be ready too, perhaps entering four floats; its celebration day was October 7. France (French-Canadians) planned to contribute two floats.

Part of the parade atmosphere would be aided by several appearances of the mounted Chicago Hussars drill team in full regalia. They would enter the grounds at 10 a.m. and give a demonstration of riding skills in the Stock Pavilion at 11 a.m. Later they would lead and guide the floats through the route described and illustrated by maps in most of the press on October 5. Floats would enter at the Sixty-second Street entrance, pass the Administration Building, circle Manufactures, pass Horticulture, Illinois, and the other state buildings before exiting back at Sixty-second Street and Stony Island Avenue.

Even without the Kansas City and St. Louis entries, the float count was 36 a week into October. A new lead float, "Genius of Music," led by Professor G. Katzenberger, was announced in the *Herald* on Saturday, October 7. Thus, although "final drawing plans" for all floats were turned in to headquarters on October 4, changes occurred in the float order and design up until parade time.

Souvenirs

Beginning September 30, souvenir tickets became available; and businesses bought them up in small and large blocks depending on the number of their employees. Demand at headquarters at 100 Washington Street mounted to the point that several outlets in the city and at the fairgrounds were established for the convenience of purchasers. Many people asked for free tickets for any number of reasons; but the committee wanted a paid-attendance record and few were granted except, for example, to parade participants and dignitaries. Chicago owed itself a salute for rebuilding, growing, and presenting the World's Columbian Exposition. Indications favored a record turnout, especially by the city residents.

The price of the child's special ticket, which had a stub and looked much like the adult 50-cent ticket, was a contentious issue. Many papers and groups repeatedly championed a 10-cent ticket for youth under fourteen years of age. The lower rate would have been a good incentive, since young people rarely furnished even a thirtieth of a day's total attendance. Fair officials discussed the idea and quieted the press by announcing that a child's ticket would be 10 cents starting on October 10. The directors and Kerr reasoned that a big crowd of adults on Monday might endanger children. The Union League Club, which had started a drive in September to collect money for buying and donating children's tickets to the needy, purchased more than 2000 tickets.

Starting October 4, the design for the souvenir "Chicago Day" badge was illustrated in many local newspapers. The cost would be one dollar, a bargain, since the minted silver half-dollar of each badge was being sold by the Exposition for the same price. Before the fair had opened, officials had requested Federal support of $5 million, but only 5 million half-dollars were struck. To make up the difference, the Exposition administration promptly sold each souvenir coin for one dollar. The badges (illustrated on page 1) became available on October 5 and enjoyed such rapid sales that Kerr's committee quickly ordered more. Ten outlets around the city were organized to promote sales.

LADIES' OUTFITTERS,

202 and 204 State Street, Corner Adams.

WE ARE TYPICAL CHICAGOANS

CHICAGO OUR PRIDE!

FREE! FREE! FREE!

WE PROPOSE TO MAKE,

CHICAGO DAY

The Red-Letter Event of the World's Fair, and to help pay off all the funds and floating indebtedness, as well as give every man, woman and child who has not seen the Fair an opportunity of seeing it on that day Free! Free! Free!

During the entire week, UNTIL SATURDAY NIGHT, INCLUDING EVENINGS until 10 o'clock, our store will be open and we shall distribute free to every purchaser A CHICAGO DAY SOUVENIR ADMISSION TICKET, good only for Oct. 9th, Chicago Day! This is Chicago liberality. Tickets will be distributed in our

CLOAK, SUIT, FUR, MILLINERY, JEWELRY, GLOVE AND CORSET DEPTS.

We place no restrictions upon this offer except that the purchase shall not be less than $3.00. Our goods are marked in plain figures. One price to all.

Advertisement in the *Chicago Daily News*, October 4, 1893

The committee finally had enough firm plans for Monday, October 9, that they laid out a 34-page souvenir program to sell for 25 cents. Changes were numerous, and it was not issued until amazingly late—October 7. Its colorful wrapper is illustrated on the front cover. Newspapers printed the committee's schedule of events in varying detail.

The Ferris Wheel Company announced that it would issue a special souvenir diploma for all patrons on Monday; the back of the certificate would show a birds-eye view of the grounds much like that seen by riders when at the top of the wheel.

A Department Store Closure, *Chicago Herald*, October 4, 1893

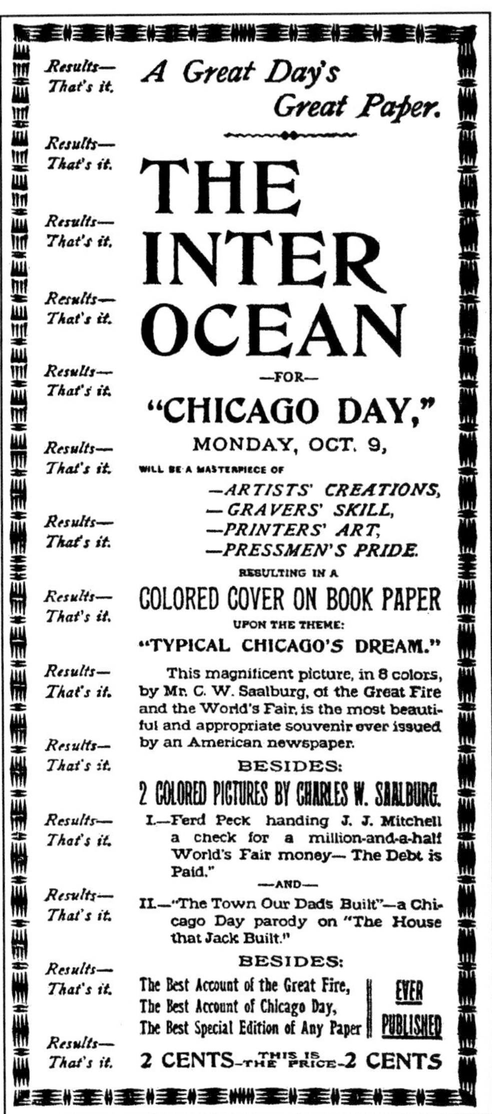

Advertisement in *Chicago Herald*, October 8, 1893

Many local newspapers, such as the *Inter Ocean*, announced that they would issue a special souvenir Chicago Day edition. The uniform and enthusiastic support and generous press space allowed for Chicago Day plans in most of the papers provided wonderful publicity for a one-day event in an already full and illustrious world's fair.

Business Closures

In ever-increasing numbers, businesses, clubs, and government agencies in Chicago were agreeing to close on Monday for the big holiday. Daily, new subscribers to this trend were listed in the newspapers. The courts would close and so would boards of exchange and Chicago clubs. Although Chicagoans worked long and hard, growing numbers of laborers were joyously going to be free to celebrate a city thanksgiving. The previous resolve of the Chicago Day committee in September was strengthened when Mayor Harrison issued his own proclamation on October 4:

> WHEREAS, The 9th day of October, 1871, the City of Chicago was visited by a deluge of fire and almost wiped out of existence, which affliction carried its name around the world as the city of modern times which had suffered the most terrible calamity; and
>
> WHEREAS, Since then Chicago has grown and prospered as no other city in the world had done in the same period of time, having added over six fold to its population and a hundred fold to its wealth; and
>
> WHEREAS, Our citizens are desirous of showing the world their gratitude for the bountiful dispensation of Providence in allowing it to prosper so abundantly and have determined the 9th

day of this month, the twenty-second anniversary of the great fire, to attend the World's Fair and make it the gala day of the Fair.

Therefore, To enable our people to evidence their gratitude to the Giver of all gifts, I, Carter H. Harrison, Mayor of Chicago, hereby request and advise all the business people of our city to abstain from work and lend their efforts towards making "Chicago day" the banner day of the World's Columbian Exposition.

Carter H. Harrison, Mayor

The mayor was a noted orator of the day and, when called upon, never lacked for words.

Governor Altgeld met with Director-General Davis on October 4, volunteering his help on Chicago Day wherever it could best be used. It was decided that Altgeld would bring his military staff.

Commercial pressures in the city would be relieved on Monday.

Transportation and Accommodations

By the end of the first week in October, all rail lines were offering one-cent-a-mile incentive rates. Most let the rates stand for ten days thus allowing distant visitors to come early, stay awhile, and still leave with the lower rates in force. Newspapers listed more and more nearby towns that planned "specials" into Chicago for the big day. Chicago depots had record heavy traffic on Saturday and Sunday, October 7 and 8, so the entire city knew that large numbers of out-of-town guests would throng the grounds.

The World's Fair Steamship Company announced that they would have twelve vessels running, including the whaleback boat *Christopher Columbus*, specially built for the Exposition. Boat capacity to the fair was listed at 16,000 passengers an hour from downtown to Casino (Exposition) Pier, which extended out from the Peristyle. On the Pier, the two-speed Movable Sidewalk, costing five cents a ride, was both transportation onto the grounds and a novel amusement.

The Whaleback Boat *Christopher Columbus*

City cable cars, horse-drawn omnibuses, and the newly constructed elevated line, the Alley "L," which went into the fairgrounds at the Transportation Building, were scheduled to run all day and into Tuesday morning or until the last reveler got home. The Alley "L" started downtown at Congress Street and ran over the alley between State Street and Wabash Avenue south to the Exposition grounds; it was also called the South-Side Elevated. The Calumet electric line at ground level came up to the fairgrounds from the south. A comfortable capacity of 500,000 people using all modes was projected, since spectators were expected to use transit facilities during all the morning hours. Some concern was reported that the evening might see a rush after the Night Pageant.

Chicago Day organizers further moved to smooth traffic by arranging to open the grounds early on Monday at 6:30 a.m. and not close until midnight, thus allowing an orderly morning entrance and evening exit after the fireworks finale.

It was not until the weekend that visitor and resident alike discovered that Chicago was full. The *Sunday Tribune* of October 8 described the crush at Dearborn, Central, Union, and other stations; extra officers were required to keep folks moving out of the stations and into the city.

CHICAGO DEPOTS	LOCATION	RAILROADS
Dearborn Station	Polk St. and 3rd Ave.	Atchison, Topeka & Santa Fe; Chicago & Erie; Chicago & Eastern Illinois; Chicago & Grand Trunk; Chicago & Western Indiana; Louisville, New Albany & Chicago ("Monon route"); New York, Lake Erie & Western; Wabash
Grand Central	5th Ave. and Harrison St.	Baltimore & Ohio; Chicago & Northern Pacific; Northern Pacific; Great Western; Wisconsin Central
Union Depot	Canal and Adams St.	Chicago & Alton; Chicago, Burlington & Quincy; Chicago, Milwaukee & St. Paul; Pittsburgh, Fort Wayne & Chicago; Panhandle Route (Pa.)
Van Buren Street Depot	Van Buren and Sherman St.	Lake Shore & Michigan Southern; Chicago, Rock Island & Pacific
Randolph Station	Foot of Lake St.	Illinois Central suburban trains
Central Depot	12th St. and Park Row	Illinois Central; Michigan Central; Chicago & West Michigan; Cleveland, Cincinnati, Chicago & St. Louis ("Big Four")
Nickel Plate Depot	Clark and 12th St.	New York, Chicago & St. Louis
Wells Street Depot	Wells and Kinzie St.	Chicago & North-Western; Milwaukee, Lake Shore & Western

The *Tribune* printed a listing of filled-to-capacity downtown hotels that they had contacted: Great Northern, Grand Pacific, Grand Union, Windsor, Saratoga, Marquette, Grace, Gore's, McCoy's, Atlantic, National, Kuhn's, Stafford's, Clifton, Wellington, Niagara, Leland, Richelieu, Victoria, Pickwick, Auditorium, University, Alton, Princess, Stag, Richmond, Lincoln, Palmer, Brevoort, Tremont, Commercial, and Briggs. They also enumerate lodging places filled to capacity in the vicinity of the fairgrounds: Edgertons, Chicago Beach, Clarksdale, Columbian, Cornell Avenue Hotel, Garfield, Harvard, Delaware, Genoa, Lemont, Endeavor, Wilovid, Mecca, Park Gate, Pullman, Grand, Barron's Suburban, Lexington, Hyde Park, Oakland, Southshore, Waukesha, Windermere, White House, Niagara, Plantation, World's Fair Inn, Yorkshire, and Vermont Hotel. The only solace the account afforded was that all hotels were putting up cots, and some still had a few available.

Special Events

The organizers sought to distribute the Chicago Day events around the park so spectators would not be tempted to congregate at just a few locations. There would be entertainment for all ages. The day's events were to span time from the 10 a.m. program opening to the finale of the fireworks, about 10 p.m. As mentioned, the fireworks would take place from the Midway to the lakeshore. Midway concessions were asked to add special decorations to attract customers, but the request went largely unheeded. State buildings would remain open late.

Aerialist Jean Weitzman would walk above the crowd on a 600-foot-long wire strung from the top of the Music Hall to the Casino. The tightrope walker and Samuel Baldwin's balloon ascension would both be high up so that all could see. Music would abound all day.

The Cloud Projector Company planned to set up its equipment east of Machinery Hall near the south end of the fairgrounds to provide entertainment and a demonstration in the evening. Portraits of world's fair dignitaries and others, the flag, stars, and the inscription "All Hail Chicago" would be some of the kaleidoscope of images projected onto the clouds. If the sky was clear, a sheet of steam would be released from boilers to serve as a screen.

The Stock Pavilion amphitheater at the south end of the park would be the scene for many events including a demonstration at 3 p.m. of lacrosse, a game of Native American origin, between a team of Iroquois and Pottawatomie Indians. Pokagon and the son of the chief who had given Chicago its name would be referees. A first-ever parade of cart horses in the Pavilion was postponed by fair officials to an unspecified date. Since retail merchants would have had the day off, hundreds of their teams had been entered in the parade. Team owners and fairgoers were disappointed.

Security

Judging by newspaper accounts, early security arrangements were nominal with much of what was planned falling to the Columbian Guard under Colonel Edmund Rice. However, as ticket sales mounted and train traffic into the city increased, especially on the weekend, expanded plans to maintain control were described in the papers. Chief of Police Brennan of the city offered 150 of his top officers to aid 1700 guardsmen with movement of spectators at the fair.

Colonel Rice of the Guard

Also, since pickpockets were the worst sort of street crime of the day and big crowds were their best environment, city police and detectives quietly rounded them up. Saturday night an order was given to bring in all well-known thieves, and the most dangerous known pickpockets were corralled and confined to "hard cells." Of the 30 arrested to October 8, sixteen were named in the *Tribune*. They were to be arraigned after Chicago Day on charges of disorderly conduct. This tactic, illegal today, was an attempt to boost public confidence and provide a trouble- and crime-free day.

Control was needed. Record crowds were arriving by rail, packing the hotels—surely a prophecy and warning for the coming Monday.

W. H. Cartwell, M.D., Columbian Guard # 1872

Weather

Ah, the weather—the maker and breaker of great plans! The weather for Chicago Day only became a concern in early October. The *Sunday Herald* of October 1 reported good attendance on a series of wet days in September; indoor exhibits especially benefited, and food concessions and the Midway shows saw extra business. Outdoor activities were dampened, but the *Herald* left the reader feeling that the World's Columbian Exposition was great "rain or shine." On the next Saturday, October 7, the *Chicago Daily News* summed up the week's attendance at the fair at just over 1,000,000 "not withstanding the unfavorable weather."

Journalists asked Kerr on October 6 for a prediction; but he said that the local bureau, headed by Professor Marvin, would not project conditions more than two days in advance; Kerr, on his own, forecast good weather. Saturday's low at the Weather Bureau exhibit near the Government Building was a chilly 43°F, but the high was a comfortable 71°F with clear skies and southeast winds at about 20 miles an hour.

Sunday's papers were more positive as a beautiful autumn day broke over Chicago; the low was 49°F, and the high, a glorious 78°F. This break in the weather led to a festive atmosphere everywhere in the city as visitors poured into Chicago and tried to find places to stay. Residents in horse-drawn carriages paraded through the streets. The October 8 Exposition attendance of over 88,000 was a Sunday record; it was small compared to weekdays, because not all exhibits were open in deference to the Sabbath. Every park, theater, and amusement in Chicago was full. Henry Irving and Ellen Terry were leads in the "Merchant of Venice" at the Columbia Theater; two Molière comedies were at Hooleys; "Evergreens" by Mrs. Burton Harrison, starring Felix Morris, was playing at the Schiller; Imre Kirafly's long-running symbolic spectacle "America" continued at the Auditorium; world traveler and author John L. Stoddard was giving stereopticon-aided lectures on Japan; "The Ensign" was at the Haymarket; "A Trip to Chinatown" had opened at the Grand Opera House; W. H. Crane's "Brother John" was presented at McVickers; and John L. Sullivan, the recently defeated champion pugilist, took the stage at the Empire Theater in "The Man From Boston." Restaurants scrambled to provide enough food and service for customers. The editorials of Sunday urged the multitudes expected Monday to be polite, good-tempered, patient, regard others, and exercise forbearance.

Scores of newspapers from around the country sent their best wishes to Chicago for a wonderful and deserved day, and these were reprinted in full for the benefit of readers.

Everything was ready for a perfect holiday in Chicago!

Newspapers issued in the early morning hours of October 9 were extravagantly illustrated souvenir editions featuring the latest information on Chicago Day from the night before. Reproductions of front pages include the *Inter Ocean* on page 3, *Tribune* on page 10, and *Herald*, page 32. Kerr's committee had moved its office down to a clubhouse on Fifty-sixth Street and East End Avenue near the grounds to make final arrangements and supervise the various Sunday practice sessions in preparation for Monday. Rail traffic on the weekend plus the promise of superb weather led to speculation that 500,000 people—a record—would enjoy Chicago Day. To prevent delays, parade and pageant personnel were urged to be at their stations in or near the park one hour earlier than originally planned. The schedule of events was printed in detail with maps for those without programs. The meaning of Chicago Day was reiterated: the anniversary of the dreadful devastation by fire in 1871, the explosive rebuilding of the city, and fighting for and hosting the grandest world's fair ever. The press continued to urge everyone to attend. Numerous facades of downtown businesses, including the *Brooklyn Eagle* paper, *Tribune*, and Mandel Brothers department store, were decorated.

J. Sterling Morton, chief of all U.S. weather bureaus, had arrived on Sunday and predicted "fair and slightly cooler" weather. Alderman Kerr and hundreds of others associated with Chicago Day called Morton and were delighted to learn his forecast for a fine day with an expected high of 72.

The big story in the special morning editions recounted, column after column, the varied tales of the large throng of visitors who could not find places to sleep the night before. Many slept on cots thrown up in hotel corridors and lobbies, creating safety and fire risks in newly rebuilt Chicago; and hotels turned away hundreds. Saloon owners rented chairs at one dollar apiece. Halls and doorways were shelter for many. Since the weather was beautiful, parks turned out to be a refuge for others. At first, policemen on the beat administered the standard treatment given to transients—a "hot foot." The soles of a prostrate sleeper's shoes were rapped smartly with a night stick until he got up and moved along. Highly effective in its day, this method could lead to charges of assault today. Soon it became apparent that there were overwhelming numbers of happy and law-abiding visitors in the parks merely waiting for Monday, and station chiefs delivered orders to leave them in peace. Police stations were opened to serve as temporary inns for as many homeless as possible. When the stations were full, the staff tried to find accommodations for those they had to turn away. Many window-shopped downtown or walked the streets. Some rode city transportation to the outskirts, usually to the north side, looking for a comfortable resting spot. Satchels became pillows. The good-humored throng, many with picnic baskets for Monday lunch at the fair, accepted the conditions graciously. Souvenir stands and food shanties along the west side of Stony Island Avenue outside the fairgrounds took people in and stayed open all night—to great financial advantage.

Horace Tucker, Chief of Admissions, had assigned his entire staff of 420 to specific jobs at the entrance booths. He had generated incentive by offering boxes of cigars to the men selling and collecting the most tickets. One concern was the expected delay that the two-piece ticket would cause, because it required the ticket taker to separate it and return the stub as a souvenir; this could take more time than the usual one-piece ticket used in the newly invented turnstiles which automatically chopped tickets.

Colonel Rice's Guard and the volunteer police also had their location assignments, which were reported in the paper. They would be at the park early. Tucker and Rice had suggested that each man

Horace Tucker

bring a generous lunch, as duty could last until the fair closed that night—a sixteen-hour day.

The celebration was underway!

THE CHICAGO HERALD.

THIRTEENTH YEAR. MONDAY MORNING, OCTOBER 9, 1893.—TWENTY PAGES. TWO CENTS.

GREATEST OF DAYS.

Chicago's Turn at the Columbian Exposition.

SPLENDID WEATHER IS ASSURED.

The Special Morning Issue of the *Herald* Printed on Chicago Day With a Bold Pink Banner

CHICAGO DAY

Before 6 a.m. on October 9, 1893, all 420 ticket sellers, ticket collectors, gate keepers, and inspectors in the employ of Superintendent of Admissions Horace Tucker arrived at Jackson Park and took their places. Ninety-five ticket sellers carried nearly 600,000 souvenir Chicago Day tickets to 68 ticket booths at 25 entrances. Twenty-five inspectors were in place to oversee ticket collectors at 187 turnstiles. Tucker had instructed them to set their alarm clocks and arrive early. They did not get there any too soon.

In the gray dawn, men worked to throw out crimson banners along the roof of the Manufactures Building. From this vantage point, they could see the crowds coming.

One man climbed to the top of the Administration Building's golden dome and watched the approach. The *Tribune* described what he saw: To the west a black mass of people poured down from the Illinois Central station, an unbroken cataract flowed down over the steps of the Elevated station, and cross-town electric cars were so loaded that they were overworked. For ten minutes he watched; and before he knew it, the crowd was there.

The gates opened on schedule at 6:30 a.m. Turnstiles clicked at a record-breaking rate, and people poured in like a stream that had broken its dam. Within one minute, the Midway Plaisance was swarming; and in the first hour 16,000 people crammed Casino Pier and its Movable Sidewalk. On the grounds, people were everywhere. Despite attempts to look military and fierce, the pretty little guides in imitation West Point outfits were ignored by the crowd. Early hours of the forenoon saw the Court of Honor choked and the thoroughfare past Fine Arts packed from Stony Island Avenue to the lakeshore.

The Weather

It is doubtful that any feature of Chicago Day was more important than the weather. Had conditions been selected, they could not have been more perfect.

At 5 a.m. there was a shade of gray in the sky; half an hour later there was a faint tinge of crimson. Soon the deepest red was replaced with fringes of yellow light that further foretold an ideal day. Then the skies were pure azure; and the White City's gilded domes and white buildings, bedecked in streamers and flags, lay in beautiful contrast against the blues of the sky, the lake, and the waterways. Breezes were just sufficiently strong to unfurl the flags of nations, and Lake Michigan lay silent. Chicago Day had dawned. It was flawless! The clean, crisp air put "go" into everything.

There was continuous sunshine after 6:55 a.m., and weather bureau instruments on the fairgrounds recorded a temperature of 58° F at 6:30 a.m., rising to a maximum of 62° between 7:15 and 9:15 a.m., after which temperatures fell slowly reaching 55° at 5 p.m. Westerly winds prevailed to 6:35 a.m., shifting at that time to northwest, and to north at 7 a.m. Northeast winds prevailed after 10:30 a.m. Another account referred to the day as having a "delicious east wind."

Folded Card With Color Weather Map

Transportation to the Fair

On a normal day, people had several choices of transportation to Jackson Park: They could ride the cable, cross-town electric, or horse cars of the Chicago City Railway; commute on the Elevated Railroad; take one of the lines of the Illinois Central; travel by boat; or walk. Residents from the north and west of Chicago first traveled downtown, then transferred for the trip to Jackson Park. This was no normal day, and all transportation facilities—both regular and improvised—groaned under the huge increase in business.

Chicago City Railway (Cable, Cross-town Electric, and Horse Cars)

Crowds from the country, many of whom had just reached the city on early trains, began traveling to the fair over the Wabash Avenue (Cottage Grove) and State Street cable cars at 5:30 a.m. Soon aisles, platforms, and footboards were filled; and the roofs were covered with people. Men and women hung out heads and arms or dangled their feet through open windows. As many as fifty men—mostly long-whiskered farmers—rode the roofs and waved their hats to the cheering onlookers; the police were powerless to stop them. Under this unusual load, the roof of one cable car broke; and its underpinning collapsed. Policemen and railway company guards compelled the packed-in passengers of the following cars to crowd over and give these passengers room. Many filled-to-capacity cars, closed to additional travelers, shut out "South-Siders" who hoped to take the cable close to their homes. These unfortunates by the thousands were forced to go downtown and begin the journey to the fair from a common starting point. Concerned about accidents, the company placed extra men at every curve and important corner. They had already brought in 100 expert gripmen from Kansas City and Omaha.

The cross-town electric intersected Jackson Park at Sixty-third Street. In the morning, fairgoers clamored for any seat they could find in or on the cars. The roofs of several were crushed, but no one was injured, and riders were simply asked to get down so that the cars could proceed to the fair.

The North-Side cable proved inadequate on Chicago Day. People clung to stanchions and railings and stood on each other inside the cars. Because the LaSalle Street tunnel would accommodate only two layers of people on running boards, the company stationed men to pull off the excess to prevent injury. If passengers showed that they could flatten themselves against the car, they were allowed to continue. The West-Side transportation congestion was worst on the Van Buren Street horse cars. There was not an inch of space or a handhold available. Some cars carried 100 people inside, plus 40 more on the roof and hanging from other places.

Alley Elevated Railroad (South-Side Rapid Transit Railroad)

Every car and engine of the Alley "L" was placed in service and ready for passengers by 6:30 a.m. But as early as 6 o'clock, people began gathering. The first crush was at the Congress Street terminal, where surrounding streets were thronged, and the stairways and elevated platform were soon packed. Supports quivered and groaned but held; however, waiting-room doors were torn from their hinges, and iron bars and glass from the ticket offices were, respectively, bent like twigs and ground to powder. Trains were quickly loaded with 1000 people—sometimes 1300 squeezed aboard—and gates were slammed in the faces of hundreds struggling to reach them. Six cars made up a train, and the trains ran two minutes apart. When packed trains stopped at intermediate stations, people waiting made desperate efforts to get on board; but only a few were successful in wedging themselves in. Hats were torn off, clothes were pulled and disheveled, and women were crushed and jostled. People at the intermediate stations waited up to two hours to board, and the vast crowds did not slacken until noon. By 2 p.m. they had again swollen to great proportions. Some people gave up and went back home; others, especially the timid and infirm, waited until the rush was over. The inventive took a train north, then secured a seat on a south-bound train at the cost of two fares (the fare was five cents, single journey). The result was that more than one train went around the loop loaded to the limit.

Illinois Central

By 6:30 a.m. fairgoers were coming from all directions; and the torrent converged downtown on the Van Buren Street viaduct where it passed over the big bridge to divide into two groups: one traveling on the Illinois Central and one riding the steamships to the fairgrounds. There was considerable scrambling at the point where the two groups divided, and some visitors who were headed for the trains were borne along with the crowd headed for the pier and compelled to go to the fair by boat, and vice versa. By 9 o'clock Michigan Avenue was filled with the masses, fighting and struggling to wedge through to the Van Buren Street viaduct; from the edge of the crowd, it took two to three hours to reach the trains. By 10 o'clock an estimated 150,000 people waited to get on the viaduct; and at all times between 7:30 a.m. and noon, there were 70,000 on the structure itself. Once on the viaduct, it took 50 minutes to board a train. Due to the forward momentum of the crowd, many people, unable to reach the ticket windows, ended up at the Illinois Central turnstiles without tickets. The company remedied the resulting delays by placing ticket sellers out in the crowd.

When the trains started running at 7 a.m., they loaded from one track and left every five minutes; by 7:45 a.m. they were loading from two tracks and leaving every three minutes; and at 8 o'clock orders went out to run the trains one minute apart. At the peak, 1000 people were transported each minute, and an estimated 115,000 were carried by these special non-stop trains from Van Buren Street to the Exposition before noon. In addition, Illinois Central suburban and through trains brought another 75,000 to the fairgrounds. Because the suburban trains, which started at the Randolph Street Station, were already full when they passed through stations nearer Jackson Park, many residents along the Illinois Central did not reach the fair until mid-afternoon.

Fairgoers on the Van Buren Street Viaduct, July 4, 1893. Larger Crowds Converged Here on Chicago Day. *(Harper's Weekly)*

By Other Railroad Lines to the Exposition

Many railroads bringing passengers into Chicago made switching arrangements whereby passengers from their downtown depots could travel directly to Jackson Park. Also, residents on the west side of Chicago could ride directly to Terminal Station on the Baltimore & Ohio and Northern Pacific.

World's Fair Steamship Company

From 8 a.m. a fleet of a dozen steamboats, including the whaleback *Christopher Columbus*—the most favored of the fleet, carried fairgoers from the Van Buren Street Pier to Casino Pier. Boats carried as many passengers as the law allowed. When they were full and the dock captain gave the signal to cast lines, it was difficult to get the gangways ashore, because hundreds of people sought to swarm over them onto the vessels; and planks were pulled back with expectant passengers still standing on them. As the good-natured crowd scurried aboard the boats, they jostled and elbowed and treaded on each other's feet but took the mishaps as evidence of friendly rivalry to be first on board and at Jackson Park. At the close of Chicago Day, boat passengers totaled an estimated 180,000.

Alternative Transportation

At least 25,000 people walked to the fair. Others arrived in an odd assortment of conveyances, even rickety ones that had rested in obscurity for years. Anyone with a conveyance that could be driven used it for hire. It was a great day for a man with a team, and every man who had a horse was on parade. The foxy iceman delivered his load early in the day and then turned his vehicle into an omnibus; although not as smooth as an electric car, it beat walking. And out on Lake Michigan from pier to pier was a string of every available craft and cruiser that would float.

How One "North-Sider" Got to the Fair

When a *Tribune* reporter inquired about one North-Sider's trip to the fair, he responded, "Well, I suppose you ask the question on account of my general dilapidated condition." He continued:

> It was 8 o'clock when I started for the Fair. The North Side cable behaved itself admirably and there was little difficulty getting downtown before 8:40. Five minutes later the Van Buren Street pier was reached. There was no possible way in reaching the Illinois Central trains for an hour, if I followed the usual pathway, there was such a crowd.

He sneaked around and took a seat in one of the empty incoming trains and was expelled.

> While I was proceeding to 'git' I happened to meet a sub-assistant to the road, a study in palmistry followed, and I was soon provided with standing room in one of the "cattle trains" and bound for the fair. All the stations were crowded as we passed along at 9:15 o'clock and all the south-bound trains were packed.
>
> Arriving at the terminal station I got into a crush around the ticket office, not having a ticket. When through I was a sight to see. I had started out robed in my best—it was "best" no longer. I had an idea I was cute—that is gone. I had an umbrella—that's gone. I had a lunch—it's gone. Had a stiff collar and a new shine—both gone. Had a determination to see Chicago day at the Fair—well, I have that yet, and you can gamble on my seeing some of it. When you remember that I was alone and took two hours to get here, possibly you can imagine how a family would make the trip.

Who Were the Fairgoers?

From all parts of the nation, the flow of Chicago Day visitors began arriving on Saturday, continued all day Sunday, and they were still arriving in record numbers on Monday. Through trains were given preference over special trains, and serious delays of some special trains meant that there were hopeful Chicago Day visitors who did not arrive until the day's festivities were over; but they stayed, determined to see the great fair. Railroad men, who were all kept overtime, knew that the crowd was larger than the most enthusiastic estimate. Freight brakemen worked on passenger trains, and all engines and passenger coaches were in service. Nearly every train entering the station carried a green flag, meaning it was followed by another.

The majority of people living within a radius of 150 to 200 miles waited until the last minute in order to take advantage of special trains that arrived early in the morning and left the same day.

Although trains had been arriving all night, the big rush began at 7 a.m. with the arrival of special trains from Indiana, Iowa, and Michigan and 25 from Illinois and Wisconsin towns. Then came the suburban trains from Lake Michigan's north shore and areas west and, finally, the vestibuled sleeping cars from the far West and East. At the railroad stations it was estimated the morning business had totaled 305,700; by 6 p.m., 350,000.

Many towns large (for example, Milwaukee) and small (for example, Beatrice, Nebraska) were almost devoid of population when fairgoers left for Chicago. Rockford, Illinois, added 3500 celebrants. From Omaha came four sections and 40 cars; from Duluth, 30 carloads; from the Dakotas, 40; from Denver, 40; and from St. Paul, 50. From the beginning of the fair, New Yorkers had the opportunity to travel on coach excursion trains; many of these passengers would not have come to the fair had they not secured the lower excursion rates. The *Herald* commented: "It was a great object lesson, unfortunately too late, showing how much larger would have been the attendance had the railroads displayed a liberal spirit from the beginning." On October 7, the St. Louis-to-Chicago fare was reduced to $6 round-trip; and an estimated 20,000 people, who otherwise would not have gone to the fair, left for Chicago.

Chicagoans, up before dawn to make their way to the fairgrounds before the out-of-towners, found their guests had already arrived. Fifty thousand people had walked the streets all night or slept in parks. And the thousands who slept on cots in hotel corridors, in chairs, and on park benches did not find their quarters conducive to late rising.

Kerr's plan for a city holiday became a reality; various firms and institutions of the city gave employees the day off from work and included tickets, conveyances, and even free lunches. Many Chicago stores and factories placed placards in their windows: "Closed for Chicago Day"; and all the big office buildings closed and placed signs on the doors: "Visitors not Allowed Today." With a few exceptions—South Water Street and Adams Street from LaSalle Street to the river—there was not much downtown decoration; the great majority of businesses showed their support by just closing their doors for the day. A group of 38 wholesale meat men off for the day comprised one of the merriest parties bound for the fair. Vigorously tooting horns with gay abandon, they rode to Jackson Park on a tallyho behind a ten-horse team and had a wonderful time together. The united fruit buyers also went down to the gates in tallyho coaches, "strewing beatific vocal discord and ham sandwiches" in their pathway. At the south end of the Basin, they climbed aboard three waiting barges and rowed about the Court of Honor and Lagoon, displaying the association's colorful banners and escutcheons.

The makeup of the crowd was different from ordinary fair attendance. In addition to country folk already mentioned, the group coming by street car and entering through Midway gates was almost entirely composed of artisans, laborers, mechanics, and small shopkeepers, who brought their wives and families, carried bulky lunch baskets, and looked bewildered. The fact that a large number of working people were in attendance was emphasized by the huge crowds in the Manufactures Building and Machinery Hall.

For a day, Chicago was the world.

Record Attendance

The attendance record at the World's Columbian Exposition had been 283,273 on July 4. The record for paid attendance for one day at any world's fair was held by the Paris Exposition of 1889—about 397,000 visitors. There was intense excitement in the air as Chicago was prepared and eager to break the Paris record.

Souvenir Chicago Day tickets had been on sale at Jackson Park and at downtown locations for over a week, but only 80,000 had been sold. On Chicago Day lines at the ticket booths were very long. Six ticket sellers in each booth kept the lines moving rapidly, but they seemed to grow rather than decrease. Predictions came true; the two-part souvenir tickets took almost twice as long to handle.

The Gathering Crowd at Terminal Plaza

Seven hundred and fifty thousand souvenir Chicago Day adult tickets had been printed. In addition to the 80,000 sold prior to Chicago Day, another 40,000 were sold downtown on Chicago Day. Approximately 26,000 of the tickets sold early at downtown ticket offices were never presented at the World's Columbian Exposition. A few tickets were sold to passengers on the Baltimore & Ohio trains. All but 5000 of the remaining were placed on sale in the ticket booths at the opening of the day.

Before noon, Tucker sent out about 50,000 regular tickets. This did not mean that all the souvenir tickets had been sold; it simply showed that the demand for tickets was so great that the gate inspectors feared running short. Ticket sellers at some gates did run short and used regular tickets, because deliveries of more souvenir tickets were delayed due to the crowds.

At 10 a.m. a ticket taker at the Sixty-fourth Street gate stopped long enough to read the figures on his turnstile; he wrote 60,000 on the back of an envelope. Tickets at that gate had always averaged one-fifth of the total returns. The man multiplied 60,000 by five and jubilantly sent a telephone message to Horace Tucker. Tucker sent out reinforcements with more boxes to stow away the shiny half-dollars, which were plentiful on Chicago Day.

At noon Tucker sent out a bulletin: "The Paris record is broken to smithereens, and the people are still coming."

At 1:30 p.m. three inspectors ran into Tucker's office. "Four hundred thousand people on the first jump!" said Tucker. He was considering setting the printing presses to work to grind out more Chicago Day tickets. Phones rang. "How many people in the park?" asked many voices. "The story up here is that Horace Tucker sold out all his tickets."

Anyone who knew enough to make a decent estimate of the crowd, knew too much to risk it; and out in the midst of the crowd itself, anybody who ventured a guess at less than a million was looked upon as not possessing the proper Chicago spirit. The *Tribune* printed: "The crowd was very proud of its own greatness. It knew it was a record-breaking crowd. ... Being an integral part of the biggest thing of its kind in the world was a new experience to most of the people, and they looked upon themselves as quite the finest exhibit at Jackson Park."

During the evening, there were constant inquiries for attendance figures. People wanted to know how big a crowd they were in, and wild estimates were readily listened to and swallowed. About 6 p.m. Tucker visited each gate to secure ticket sales estimates from each seller. Based upon this information, he announced expected total admissions to reach 700,000.

As promised, Tucker rewarded men who sold and collected the greatest number of tickets. Boxes of cigars were won by a ticket seller, L. E. Decker, at the Fifty-seventh Street entrance who sold 17,843 tickets and a ticket collector, Gus Jones, at the west end of Midway Plaisance who took in 16,528. The ticket seller, a nephew of Buffalo Bill Cody, had had eight years of experience at the gates of "Buffalo Bill's Wild West" show. The winning ticket collector was an old-time circus man who had sold tickets several seasons for P. T. Barnum.

L. E. Decker, Fastest Ticket Seller

Rules of the Bureau of Admissions and Collections provided that ticket sellers and gate keepers were to work in shifts of three hours each. The first shift was usually relieved at 11 a.m., the next at 2 p.m., and so on, to the hour of closing. The number of tickets sold was usually known within two hours after the shift had been relieved. The unprecedented rush of Chicago Day visitors changed all the rules. When 11 a.m. came, Tucker found he had no men to relieve those on duty, and they were told to stay at their posts until a lull came or until the park closed for the night. At closing, the weary men had been on duty from 6 a.m. on Monday to 1 a.m. Tuesday morning.

At the Department of Admissions in a separate room especially designed for it, the tickets were counted by a force of 18 girls standing at long tables. At 1:45 a.m. on October 10, a tally revealed there had been an astounding 713,646 paid admissions—682,587 adults and 31,059 children. These were the bold-type figures printed in the papers later that morning. Add to this 37,380

Gus Jones, Fastest Ticket Taker

passes, and total entries of 751,026 were reported. In addition, Captain W. L. DeRemer, head of the ticket sellers, believed thousands of people got in free by climbing fences along the Midway Plaisance and along the south end of the grounds. Others sneaked in when the gates were opened to allow the evening parade to enter.

After the attendance figures had gone to press, four boxes of ticket stubs were found in the treasurer's office. They had come from the Sixty-second Street gate. The men who had gone to the gate in the patrol wagon found these boxes of tickets so heavy they mistook them for money and delivered them to the treasurer's office, where they were stowed away under the impression they contained silver. Once these were added to the count, Tucker's bulletin of October 11 finalized the official count at 716,881 paid admissions plus 45,060 passes for a grand total of 761,942 at Jackson Park on Chicago Day!

In modern times, it was the biggest crowd ever paying to celebrate a single event. For the largest crowd ever assembled, the *Tribune* looked back 2000 years to the march of 5,283,220 souls through tight corridors under orders of King Xerxes of Persia and concluded that not since that time had so many been gathered in so limited a space as they were in Jackson Park for Chicago Day.

What became of 40,000 leftover souvenir tickets and hundreds of thousands of stubs? The stubs were burned in the "crematory"—Horticultural greenhouse boilers—on Friday, October 13. The last mention of the unused tickets appeared in the *Tribune* on October 12: "Some disposition other than burning may be made of the unsold souvenirs." Today, an intact adult Chicago Day ticket is relatively common. They come either from the leftover 40,000 or from approximately 26,000 purchased but never redeemed at the Exposition. It is less common to find an unused child's ticket. Fifty thousand were printed; and no more than 32,000 were sold, which left 18,000 or fewer in circulation in 1893. Today's collectible market reflects this availability, and the price ratio between child and adult tickets is about six.

The immense crowds at the transportation facilities did not perceptibly thin down until past noon, and it was long after that before conveyances ceased to carry maximum loads. Those arriving from the city, reinforced by trains coming from the country, resulted in an increasingly dense crowd on the fairgrounds; by mid-afternoon, the throng was the greatest of the day. The heavy incoming traffic continued until 4 p.m., when many, fearing the night jam, started for home. It was late afternoon before weary and hungry gatekeepers found time to eat the food that had been brought to them. Their respite was brief; between 5 and 7 p.m. a second onslaught was inaugurated by sightseers of the night. Every employee in the Department of Admissions was pressed into service and remained at his post until the gates closed.

Ferris invited a *Herald* reporter to ride his great wheel; the reporter described the grand sight:

> As the car slowly lifted, the vast multitude down the street toward the Woman's Building appeared one solid mass of black, with here and there a waving plume. ... A moment later, as the car rose, the solid mass of black broke into rounded particles, and then, suddenly, with a change that was startling in the extreme, the human field below became a sea of white globes. Nine hundred and ninety-nine of every 1000 men and women in the tremendous throng were gazing upward at the moving mass of steel and iron. Their faces came so suddenly out of the solid black as to draw cries of astonishment from everybody in the car. It was as though a curtain had been suddenly drawn from over a field of white daisies of great size. ... The street, both to the westward and eastward, was one grand parade ground.

And Mr. Ferris declared, "There must be a million people down there."

So many descriptions of the crowd referred to a black sea of humanity. While the density of the crowd contributed, the description was also quite literal, since fashion's favored colors for the late fall of 1893 were black, black, and black. Women were encouraged to put all their old clothes in one dye pot, and it appears they did.

Many news articles described a well-dressed throng and spoke of the utmost good nature of the fairgoers. The *Herald* described the reigning good fellowship: "The ditch digger bumped against the millionaire and both laughed and apologized; man of letters and Bridgeport laborer stepped on one another's toes with perfect good feeling except as to the toes; brothers and sisters from the rural districts became tangled in a crush and rearranged their clothing and hats without a murmur. In the restaurants the high and the low sat down together, and if one committed a solecism the other looked toward the ceiling." It was a great democratic party in which most were well and happy. But, as will be shown, there were a few push-and-shove altercations during the day and many more in the evening when people had become weary and short-tempered.

If people were raindrops, Chicago was soaked.

Revenue and Fair Debt Closure

The ticket sellers had collected money so rapidly and were so busy that they could not make their usual daily deliveries. At 2 p.m. the first transfer of money from the ticket booths to Exposition Treasurer Anthony F. Seeberger's office was made by two patrol wagons—one an ambulance with wire grating over the windows. The wagons carried four men inside, two more on the driver's box, and a squad of armed Columbian guards around the outside. One wagon took in all the stations north of Sixty-second Street, including the Midway Plaisance booths, while the other went down the line toward Cheltenham Beach. One of the cashiers who went out in the patrol wagons said, "In some of the little booths, the ticket sellers were standing ankle deep in bills and silver. The money piled up on their counters so high that they were evidently afraid to leave it in sight, for they swept it off on the floor, and when we came along we literally scooped it up and hauled it away in bags. No attempt was made to count the money as it was taken from the booths. We simply labeled the bags and drove back to the office." Both wagons returned laden with bags of silver and boxes of bills. They were busy hauling money for the rest of the day; the last collections were made after midnight.

Seeberger selected six of his best men and put them in charge of the count. A dozen or more additional clerks were pressed into service. At 3 p.m. they began; and as the money was dumped on counters, the clerks went right to work counting, stacking up piles of silver, and making bricks of the currency. A dozen Columbian guards, all ex-regular soldiers, stood about the walls. Wearing a cartridge belt with 40 rounds of ammunition, each was armed with a Springfield rifle. By 9 p.m. the burglar-proof safes were jammed full of $5,000 packages of bills. At midnight the counters commenced to cord up $1,000 packages and place them on shelves in the iron vaults where Seeberger kept the books of the fair. At 2 a.m. tons of silver were yet to be stacked up in piles and the count verified. The clerks were ordered to stay on duty all night. Some stretched out on desk tops for a few moments rest, but all hands were at work at 6 a.m. when 20 clerks tackled the remaining pyramids of silver. All day long the clinking of coins could be heard in the corridors around Seeberger's office. At 9 p.m. on October 10, they finished. Ticket receipts at the gates on Chicago Day, independent of all sales downtown, had been $350,784.25! Of this amount, more than $75,000 was in $1 and $2 bills, a much larger sum in $5 and $10, and over three tons of silver. The clerks had stood at their posts over 36 hours without appreciable rest, getting the money ready for deposit at the bank in the Administration Building. From there it was transferred to a downtown bank.

Since it was easier to stack and count bills and it was more costly to haul coins than bills, ticket sellers had been instructed to give people coins in change whenever possible; this accounted for the predominance of paper money. The Exposition Company had a contract with an express company to haul receipts to downtown banks; it cost 20 cents to haul $1000 in bills, 35 cents to haul the same amount in silver.

Did the bank balance the morning of October 9 justify Seeberger's writing a check for over one-and-a-half million dollars? No, but with confidence the shortfall would be made up during the day, Seeberger signed a $1,565,310.76 check representing the last payment with accrued interest on issued bonds. The check was payable to the Illinois Trust & Savings Bank, as trustee for the bondholders. (A souvenir facsimile of the check is illustrated on the back cover.)

All other creditors had been satisfied the previous week, and now there was not one unpaid voucher on Seeberger's desk. At the end of Chicago Day, there was $165,000 in the bank at the Administration Building—the first money that belonged to the Exposition. They planned to put that money away to meet expenses of tearing down the Exposition, and they hoped for $1,500,000 by the end of the fair. Because the banks were closed on Chicago Day, the check lay in Seeberger's strongbox until it could be delivered to bank president John J. Mitchell, trustee for the bondholders, with modest formality the next morning.

The Inter Ocean

ILLUSTRATED SUPPLEMENT.

MONDAY OCTOBER 9, 1893.

THE EXPOSITION OUT OF DEBT.

Ferd W. Peck, Chairman of the Finance Committee, handing check for $1,333,350.00 and interest to John J. Mitchell (Trustee for the bondholders), being payment in full for issue of $5,000,000 of World's Fair Bonds.

The *Inter Ocean* Illustrating Payment of the Exposition Debt (Original in Color)

Souvenirs

Souvenir tickets to the fair had fallen into the hands of speculators, who seemed to have an unlimited supply and reaped a harvest. Among other places, they stationed themselves at the viaduct downtown and at entrances to the Exposition gates where they attracted the attention of visitors who preferred a higher price to a protracted wait in line. Speculators called, "It'll take you half an hour to get to the windows," and otherwise enticed people to "buy now and avoid the rush." They did a good business—making 10, 15, and 25 cents or more—on each ticket they sold. The *Tribune* reported that very few farmers were caught by this scheme and surmised that the farmers could wait to get to the windows because their time was not so valuable.

Thousands of the multitude wore Chicago Day badges. (A badge is illustrated on page 1.) Initially 20,000 were made, and they sold for $1 each. By 2 p.m. on Chicago Day, the last badge was sold from the stand inside the Administration Building. Then at a late hour, arrangements were made for making 5000 more. They were ready by 5 p.m. and sold out before the Night Pageant started. According to the *Tribune*, speculators who had already amassed a comfortable sum from the sale of Chicago Day tickets, dealt in Chicago Day badges at the uniform price of $2 each. The *Herald* reported many "private sales" were made at prices ranging from $1.50 to $2.50. By the next day, wily street fakers, who had bought up a number of badges, were selling them for up to $3.50. Plans were made to manufacture more and have them for sale in downtown jewelry stores for $1 by October 12.

Another indication of the intense interest in Chicago Day was the sale of a record number of issues of the *Tribune*'s Chicago Day souvenir edition—208,671 copies had been sold by 10 a.m. on October 9. Never had a Western newspaper approximated this number. Only 150,000 of the copies contained a colored picture of Ogden House.* The demand was not exhausted even when the papers were; then copies brought handsome premiums of 5, 10, and sometimes 50 cents.

Security

With the exception of pickpockets, the day was exceptionally free of disturbers—those who might have entered the grounds to deliberately cause trouble; and not a serious incident occurred. Early in the morning, a number of thieves began to crowd into cable cars and the Elevated and made special effort to secure booty in the neighborhood of the fairgrounds. Within Jackson Park, a few pickpockets—most of whom tried to ply their calling in the Fisheries Building—were caught by secret service detectives in Captain Bonfield's command. In spite of earlier arrests, Chicago Day was still a busy one for thieves; and most of the police work entailed rounding up an additional 80 pickpockets and throwing them behind bars, where they remained until they appeared in police court the next day, October 10.

The good-natured fairgoers were no problem for the police, who were reasonably well prepared for the rush. But so many of Chicago's police officers were called to handle Chicago Day crowds that it was feared burglars would be busy in outlying districts where many houses were left unoccupied. On subsequent days, no newspaper reported problems; so, by implication, the concern proved unfounded.

Chicago Day was not a day for babies and small children. In fact, the *Daily News* said it was "so much no fun" for the very young they looked as if they might live to vigorously say so some day. They were bumped, dragged through suffocating seas of knees and umbrella handles, scolded, deceived by promises not kept and appetites unappeased. Some fairgoers accused parents who took children to the fair of being unintentional and unthinking criminals.

Around the headquarters of Officer-of-the-Day Paxton, lost children were numerous. Sixty-six were picked up by the Columbian Guard. Awaiting their parents, they filled up every chair at headquarters. Newspaper tallies varied, but the next morning each printed the names of up to 19 lost children who had spent the night in the care of the officer-of-the-day. The captain, who had cared for them through the night, was quite unhappy with services rendered at the Children's Building. By noon on Tuesday, all children had been claimed.

The fire department under Chief Edward Murphy was well prepared for Chicago Day; earlier the Cold Storage Building had burned, costing lives. Concerned about fires, fair authorities kept the fireworks away from buildings; and for Chicago Day, all was calm. No account mentioned the fire department or fires at the fair.

Feeding the Multitude

Fairgoers possessed phenomenal appetites. The urgent and continuous demand for something to eat manifested itself early. By 7 a.m. the lunch counters were doing a brisk business. Thousands of fairgoers carrying picnic baskets or lunch boxes arrived at Jackson Park. At the noon hour, Wooded Island, the lakefront, and the lawns—especially in front of the Art Palace, around the Colorado, Michigan, Wisconsin, Ohio, Nebraska, North Dakota, and Kansas Buildings—were transformed into a grand picnic ground. "Keep off the grass" signs were disregarded; and in honor of the day, Colonel Edmund Rice ordered his Columbian guards not to prevent people from sitting on the grass. The park was dotted with picnickers who spread newspapers or tablecloths and ate lunches from home or from food boxes sold outside the grounds. The restaurateurs recognized that it would have been impossible to feed the crowd had it not been for those with lunch baskets; so for the first time since the fair

"All Signs Fail in Fair Weather"

* Mahlon D. Ogden's wood mansion which miraculously survived the fire of 1871.

opened, some of the established eating places were liberal enough to supply them with milk and coffee.

Thousands who were on their way to the Exposition during the lunch hour stopped to eat before they arrived in the area. Many who waited in vain hope of reaching Jackson Park gave up in despair and ate their picnic lunches wherever they could find a comfortable spot. Thousands of others took the opportunity to eat at neighboring hotels, cafes, or lunch counters in the blocks surrounding the entrances.

The hundreds of thousands who where already on the Exposition grounds without lunch baskets depended on getting something to eat at the various restaurants at the fair. They had to endure long waits and take what they could get. The morning's activities ended about noon; from then until 2 o'clock, the rush on the eating places was intense. Crowds stood among tables and behind chairs of the diners, sometimes in such numbers that waiters could not get through with orders. Some hungry visitors stood and ate; hundreds went from one restaurant to another in a vain quest for faster service. After 2 p.m. nearly every lunch counter was cleaned out of its original stock.

The restaurants were reasonably well prepared with quantities of food for the multitude, and most of them had doubled their help for the day. The Wellington Catering Company, which had eight restaurants and forty lunch counters, fed more people than all other concessions combined. It laid in stock sufficient to feed 300,000 people: 40,000 pounds of meat, 2 carloads of potatoes, 12,000 loaves of bread, 200,000 ham sandwiches, 400,000 cups of coffee, 4000 half-barrels and 3600 bottles of beer, 15,000 gallons of ice cream, and pies and cakes by the wagon-load. The company was prepared to serve 22,000 people at one time. And it did—over and over again.

The Casino Restaurant expected to serve 25,000 before midnight; and when it opened its doors at 11:30 a.m., it had on hand 100 forty-pound roasts, 50 lambs, 100 hams, 100 tongues, 400 pounds of sweetbreads, 400 pounds of "red hots," 250 gallons of soup, 1000 loaves of bread plus a huge supply of rolls, 120 gallons of ice cream, 200 pounds of cake, and 400 gallons of coffee.

There were also restaurants in the Administration, Electricity, Horticulture, and Woman's Buildings, as well as White Horse Inn, California, French Bakery, Philadelphia, Swedish, Polish, Banquet Hall Café, New England Clam Bake, Hayward's, Marine Café, several Public Comfort cafes, and Kentucky Café in the Kentucky Building. The restaurants on the Midway Plaisance fed as many people as they could attend to. In addition, the Illinois commissioners served lunch to a large number of special guests in the Illinois Building, and the New York commissioners did likewise in the New York Building.

Fruit stands scattered here and there were liberally patronized and restocked. Customers were served regardless of the quality of the fruit. Peanut and popcorn stands also dotted the fairgrounds.

Water was in demand. The public fountains were surrounded by thirsty crowds, and many were unable to get enough to drink. An enterprising boy sold ice water from a tin bucket and pocketed many nickels. There were tea stands, soda water concessions, and the many Hygeia Spring Water concessions sprinkled throughout the park, selling water at one cent a glass. Hygeia sold 500,000 glasses of water on Chicago Day and employed half a dozen young women who were still counting and bunching bushels of pennies on Tuesday.

Throughout the day, beer-wagons cavorted among thousands of people. They were greeted everywhere by thirsty fairgoers and caused quite a stoppage in traffic, but dispensing liquor was not permitted outside eating establishments. Mayor Carter H. Harrison was late for the noon Liberty Bell festivities, described later, because a beer-wagon got between him and liberty.

At dinnertime, the noon-hour scenes were repeated but with greater intensity. When all those who had eaten their basket lunches were added to those who had continued to arrive without preparations, the demand for an evening meal was twice as great as it had been at noon. Those fortunate enough to get inside a restaurant had great difficulty getting back out after they had eaten.

Some Wellington counters ran short or out of food because dense crowds delayed supply wagons. Although it contained other reports to the contrary, the *Tribune* said at one point that as far as could be determined, not a single place with food had entirely run out by day's end; and although it was a herculean task to feed the throng, nobody with patience went without a meal. The *Herald*'s report was decidedly negative: Restaurants were swamped, their kitchens inadequate, and many people were turned away unfed. Probably the truth lies somewhere in the middle: The very patient and hardy person ate supper; those whose strength gave out in the wait went without but could have sustained themselves with popcorn, peanuts, and fruit.

By order of Exposition President Higinbotham, the Manufactures Building closed at 6 p.m. This shut off the usual and best-known entrances to 18 of the Wellington Company's best patronized lunch counters. Despite pleas from the company that revenues of four to five thousand dollars would be lost, the order stood; and at 6 o'clock the Columbian guards drove everybody out of the great building and shut the doors. Because they were seldom used, few people knew about the outside entrances to the eateries, and business was slack. Wellington closed the rest of its counters at 9 p.m. Meanwhile other places were forced to close early, because they lacked further provisions.

Restaurants and pavilions on the Midway, crowded early and late, did a record-smashing business. Some of them were "eaten out" early in the day despite extra provisions. In the evening a jolly crowd of people threw care to the wind and stopped to eat and drink to pass time while waiting for some diminution in the vast throng lined up for transportation home. Restaurants were to close at 11 p.m.; it was the rule. To enforce it, about a dozen Columbian guards went into the "Original Café" at 11:15 p.m. The Café was serving about 100 patrons at the time, and the waiters resisted attempts at closure. A battle ensued between waiters and guards. Waiters threw heavy beer mugs; guards volleyed bar chairs. Patrons tried to flee; but with the fight taking place between them and the doorway, they took refuge under the tables instead. The disturbance attracted a large crowd in the street. Several of the guards were gashed and bruised; none of the waiters were hurt. The guards left, returned with reinforcements, closed the restaurant, and left again with five prisoners in tow.

Medical Care

Dr. John E. Owen

Dr. John E. Owen headed the medical department. He was in charge of the 24-bed Emergency Hospital, which comprised one-fourth of the Service Building, and two sub-hospitals located at the east end of Midway Plaisance and at Guard Station No. 7 between Machinery Hall and Terminal Station. Medical services were free. From 9 a.m. five ambulances under Owen's direction made hurried trips around the grounds, but most of the transported patients had only mild ailments or preferred the ride to walking to Emergency Hospital. The *Tribune* reported that toothaches, cramps, bad colds, headaches, and other minor complaints kept the medical staff busy until late at night; it was not a day for sickness; and "if there had been no hospital on the grounds, nobody would have suffered greatly." That report may have been made early in the day because the *Herald* had a different story: The scenes at the hospital and its courtyard between 8 and 10 p.m. were sad, exciting, and tragic. The arrival of patients was rapid; ambulances rolled up only minutes apart with most of the patients unconscious. Although deaths were few, the whole scene was deathly. The sitting rooms were filled with women who came to look after their relatives, and who looked more dead than alive themselves. Cabs took those who had convalesced to their homes, hotels, boarding houses, or other hospitals. The only overnight patient at Emergency Hospital was a middle-aged woman who developed paralysis while sightseeing. Her admission broke the Exposition's rule: "No patient shall be permitted to remain overnight." It was an emergency facility only.

The *Herald* complained of the lack of information released about patients: "The policy of Director Owen is that it is no newspaper's business who is killed or injured in Jackson Park. To all inquiries of reporters he returned dilatory or petulant replies." A *Daily News* reporter inquired about the paralyzed woman who had been admitted overnight and said Dr. Owen suddenly broke into a tirade of abuse, using the most shocking profanity. His voice was husky, his eyes bloodshot, as he announced with many oaths that he was not giving out information on people brought to the hospital. The reporter benevolently wrote that the work of Chicago Day may have disturbed the doctor's nerves.

It was reported that by 11 p.m. there had been around 108 ambulance calls, bringing 180 to 200 people to the hospital. The next morning one report was that 224 people had been treated; another said 360. In any case, it had been a very busy day at Emergency Hospital.

Accidents

The total of killed and injured persons named in the *Daily News*, *Herald*, and *Tribune* was five killed and twenty-four injured on Chicago Day. Not one of those crushed in Jackson Park during the evening exodus was listed. Of the five fatalities, two occurred in Jackson Park and three outside the fairgrounds. One man fell down the steps of the Intramural Railway and died at Emergency Hospital of a "stroke of apoplexy." A 21-year-old pyrotechnics employee died at Emergency Hospital after literally being blown apart when a fireworks mortar misfired. Outside Jackson Park, a man was killed by a West Madison Street cable car when he stepped in front of one car that had stopped but failed to observe a car coming from the other direction; another man was killed on Lincoln Avenue when he jumped off the wrong side of a cable car onto tracks and was struck by a car coming from the other direction; and a third man was run over by a wagon at Erie and Ada Streets and died at the county hospital. That only two persons were killed of the 1,612,629 passengers carried is a tribute to the transit systems in operation between downtown and the fair.

Serious accidents in Jackson Park were few: A man fell through a hole in the Movable Sidewalk shattering his wrist and injuring his head when he landed on timbers six feet below, a ticket inspector broke his leg when he jumped from the Court of Honor bandstand, a woman's foot was severed when she was crowded off the platform of the Illinois Central and a train passed over her ankle, a fainted woman was struck in the face by a ladder wielded by a man who at the same time assaulted her brother, and a woman had her foot crushed by a wheelbarrow. Many were hurt in the swarm at the corner of Manufactures Building during the evening parade of floats. At one point, so many women suffered that Russian officials opened their nearby offices as an improvised hospital and volunteer "nurses" administered care to 12 of the most seriously injured.

The majority of the injuries that occurred away from Jackson Park were due to crowded conditions on cable cars. Five men and three women fell either getting off or trying to board the cars, and their injuries were fractures, wheel-amputation of limbs, head injuries, or some combination of these. Three men were knocked down by cable cars and suffered head injuries. Four were injured at the Alley "L" and were treated for cuts, bruises, broken nose, and trampling; in addition, many women swooned and were revived. The fashionable tightly-corseted woman was more likely to faint when crushed, since her circulation was already compromised. Also away from Jackson Park, one man sustained head injuries when he was struck by a Panhandle switch engine; recovery was judged doubtful for a seven-year-old boy who was taken home with spinal injuries after being struck by a Michigan Central train; a man and woman fell and sprained their ankles, the man was unconscious; and a woman sustained head injuries when she was run down by a horse and buggy. Amazingly, many of the seriously injured were just sent home.

Permanent Attractions and Exhibits

Movable Sidewalk

From sun-up, the Movable Sidewalk on Casino Pier carried a maximum number of passengers—5600 at a time. It ran at three miles an hour on the outside loop and six on the inside loop. According to the *Tribune*, with all seats filled and people hanging on the posts, one of the motors burned out, and for the hour and a half needed for repairs, the first-ever people mover limped along at half speed on the remaining motor—three miles an hour. The *Daily News* account went like this: "It shivered an instant, jerked, and then stood as still as the Spectatorium* and no human or invented power could start it up again."

Intramural Railway

The Intramural railroad, which transported visitors about the grounds, doubly broke all its previous records on Chicago Day—125,000 were carried.

Electric Launch and Navigation Co.

The Electric Launch sold rides on the Jackson Park lagoons and canals. With ticket receipts of $12,000, the company about doubled its usual daily sales.

North Loop of the Intramural Railway**

Columbia Rolling Chair Company

The dense crowds hurt business at the Columbia Rolling Chair Company, which rented wheelchairs. The company's manager later said he could not comprehend why anybody rented a chair on Chicago Day unless the renter just wanted to sit in it, for it was impossible to get through the crowds. About 50 of their 2400 chairs became stranded and were abandoned by the renters, who thereby forfeited the two-dollar security deposit.

Midway Plaisance

Concessionaires on Midway Plaisance believed that the jam there was so great that many people who wanted to gain entrance to the various concessions and shows could not. They had a more profitable day on October 10—North Dakota and Firemen's Day, which had the second largest crowd during the Exposition due to people extending their stay past Chicago Day. Those Midway concessions that did better the day after Chicago Day were the Ferris Wheel, Ostrich Farm, Samoans, Java Village, Moorish Palace, Lapland, Dahomey, and Cairo Street. None of these had any difficulty handling what they could get of the Chicago Day crowd; and the manager of the Ferris Wheel said, although they experienced some problem with people outside their gates, after the patrons got in, there was no trouble handling them. They ran the Wheel "quicker" than usual and carried nearly 39,000.

State Buildings

Those states that especially decorated their buildings with banners, flags, and buntings for Chicago Day were Colorado, Idaho, Illinois, Indiana, Iowa, Kansas, Louisiana, Minnesota, Michigan, North Dakota—which was preparing for its day on October 10, Ohio, Pennsylvania, South Dakota, Washington, Wisconsin, and the United Territories (Arizona, New Mexico, and Oklahoma). There were constant streams of visitors to the state buildings throughout the day, and in the evening they were illuminated and filled with people. All these buildings were to stay open until midnight; but by that time, most of the visitors had left the Exposition grounds.

Newspapers took pride in describing the important Illinois Building in great detail.*** Two thousand Japanese lanterns hung outside—pendant on ropes from pillars to trees. Atop a flagstaff on the dome floated a red, white, and blue pennant with the word "Illinois" emblazoned on its side in large black letters. From the apex of the dome to either end of the roof of the structure were stretched ropes on which fluttered miniature representations of banners of the various nations of the world. All around the base of the dome and along the eaves of the building 4000 flags were draped, while from

---

* The shell of the uncompleted Chicago theater building; one of the many victims of the depression of 1893.

** See candid photograph #17.

*** See candid photograph #25.

the cornices and window ledges and over various doorways was suspended an immense amount of red, white, and blue bunting, and large flags that fluttered in the breeze over the heads of the multitudes constantly passing in and out. Inside there was bunting everywhere, and the exhibits had been specially brightened and rejuvenated. Illinois was the only state to follow the example of the Federal Government, and nearly the entire state exhibit was confined to the Illinois Building rather than dispersed throughout various departmental buildings. Agriculture (grasses and grains) and some horticulture (vegetables) were the exceptions. Therefore in the Illinois Building, and appearing striking from the overhanging galleries, the horticulture department was decorated with "Chicago" and the dates "1871" and "1893" in black concord grapes nestled in a background of white muscatels. In the department of floriculture, "Chicago" in floral lettering two feet high appeared over the south and west entrances.

All day, constant activity took place in the Illinois Building. According to the *Herald*, "It seemed as if every man, woman, and child who ever lived in Illinois and all those who now live within the confines of the state were visitors at the building. Locomotion was at times impossible and throughout the day and night was laborious." The Illinois Board of World's Fair Commissioners received and entertained many prominent citizens from various parts of the state. Governor Altgeld and the Board served luncheon to about 600 invited guests. In spite of the bustling crowds, there was one quiet place in the Illinois Building—Memorial Hall in the north wing. Here were gathered the torn, blood-soaked, burned, and tattered battle flags—labeled and numbered—borne by the Illinois regiments in the Civil War. The reverent guests were greeted by two silent sentinels and two portraits—Abraham Lincoln and Ulysses S. Grant. At night, the Illinois Building was brightly illuminated; and especially invited Chicago Day guests viewed the parade from balconies and windows.

The Pennsylvania Building—called Independence Hall—drew a large crowd eager to see the old Liberty Bell decorated in little flags and yards of bunting. The front and sides of the building were covered with shields and flags from the roof to the ground, and at the front door hung two great "Stars and Stripes" drawn aside like a curtain and making an impressive entrance. In the evening, the verandahs surrounding the building were filled with invited guests.

New York made no attempt to decorate its building; but its commissioners were active all day receiving, entertaining, and feeding prominent guests. New York was preparing for its own big day—Manhattan Day, October 21—and would benefit from Chicago Day, as floats were reused and some of the bands retained. The New Yorkers allowed hundreds of people to eat lunch on their roof, and those who had no lunches with them were served sandwiches and coffee by the caterer of the building's restaurant. At night, the building was illuminated inside and out; and during the parade, masses of people were banked against its great white walls.

The New York State Building

Although the Californians did not decorate, they participated in the celebration by sending baskets of grapes, peaches, and pears to the officers of the Exposition and serving state wines to California Building visitors. During the evening's pageant of floats, they gave up all the prime seating in their building to friends of the World's Columbian Exposition Company. Louisiana, Missouri, and Utah gave up the most advantageous locations on their verandahs and windows to sightseers; and the raised lawn in front of the Massachusetts Building offered a comfortable viewing place for thousands.

October 9 was also Florida Day. Originally scheduled for September 13 by Florida's national commissioners, the fete fizzled. The state commissioners tried again on October 9 and carried out their plans with success: The Florida Building was bustling with addresses, speeches, and orchestral music. State wine was dispensed. More than 36,000 people passed through Florida's building that day.

Foreign Buildings

Nearly all of the foreign buildings flew an American flag for the day and decorated their entrances with bunting representing their nations' colors alongside those of the United States. The Japanese in their miniature Hoo-den cottages on Wooded Island kept open house all day. India, not to be outdone, arrayed itself in golden-threaded splendor and chanted apostrophes. China burnt itself into the atmosphere in fireworks; and, according to the *Daily News*, "the haughty disrobed court of the cannibal Islands [sic] was one vast oleaginous smile from sunrise until midnight." The Swedish Building was temporarily closed, because its insurance had been canceled.

Woman's Building

The Garden Café on the top floor of the Woman's Building issued a special four-page menu with a colored cover for Chicago Day. (The menu's cover is illustrated on page 1.) The Board of Lady Managers held a special meeting in the building on Chicago Day.

Children's Building

Although it had no provision for care through the night, the Children's Building had a baby-checking department; and it did a lively business on Chicago Day. In the afternoon, many parents who had lost their claim checks were required to wait and take the babies left after those holding checks had been supplied. By the end of the day, all infants were happily matched with their families.

World's Congresses

Because of the intense interest in all the special activities taking place around Jackson Park, very few people attended sessions of the World's Congresses downtown. The programs were carried out as scheduled, since speakers had come from all over the world and could not be rescheduled. The *Tribune* reported that the 60 persons who attended the Evangelical Alliance were "lost in a sea of chairs in the Hall of Columbus."

Chicago Day Program

Chicago Welcomes the World in Music and Song

The morning's activities were to begin at 10 a.m. with a cannon "Salute to All Nations," Battery D, Lieutenant F. Russell commanding. According to an article in the *Jamestown Daily Alert*, the salute was fired over the lakefront as the Hussars made their tour of the grounds. Since the Hussars were delayed, it follows that the cannon salute was delayed; and the program was off to a late start.

"Awaiting the Signal"

Flanking the Court of Honor, trumpeters from Fort Sheridan, dressed like buglers of a royal court, heralded the day. Four were stationed on the Columbus Arch at the center of the Peristyle and four each on Manufactures, Administration, and Agriculture. No two of their costumes were the same, but all were resplendent in color and style and represented some era of medieval history. Starting a little after 11 a.m., they played a short fanfare of peace, first in quartets and then in unison, to give music to the motto, "Peace on earth, good will to men." The music was written especially for this occasion by noted composer and Chicago native Silas G. Pratt, Chicago Day program director; the verse was composed by Major Baird.

As the blare of the trumpets died away, the crowd at Terminal Plaza listened to music by the Iowa State Band. The program was opened with Richard Wagner's "Rienzi" overture, the crowd packed so tightly around the musicians that those next on the program could not make their way to the platform.

Four hundred members of the Apollo Club and 800 to 900 members of the Columbian Chorus were expected to sing "The Star Spangled Banner." Of this number, perhaps two-thirds were able to force their way to the stand through the constantly growing crowd. Intended to keep the crowd back, a rope was drawn around the stand for 25 feet on each side; but it proved a failure when people were driven over the ropes and even into the seats reserved for the singers. There was not enough room for those who were in Terminal Plaza; but once in, they could not get out, so there was no possibility of leaving before the last piece. Professor W. L. Tomlins directed the chorus; Michael Brand's 40-piece Cincinnati Band formed the orchestra. The chorus and band were at variance; but patriotism was contagious, and members of the crowd increasingly joined in singing. By the third verse, their voices drowned out the instruments. The national anthem was followed by "American Hymn," "Watch on the Rhine," "The Battle Hymn of the Republic," and other songs of national and international flavor.

"Fanfare of Universal Peace"

At the end of the third verse of the "Battle Hymn," a cry went out across the crowd announcing the arrival of the Chicago Hussars preceded by the Elgin Band. Terminal Plaza was practically impassable, and it was only after diligent work on the part of the outriders of the Hussars that a path was cleared for them to make their way from the Plaza to the Stock Pavilion for their exhibition. After allowing this procession to pass, the crowd rushed into the open space behind it and continued accompanying the chorus in "Home Sweet Home" and the finale, "America."

Noon Ringing of the New Liberty Bell and Speeches

As the musical program ended, a mighty shout from the crowd announced the discovery of Mayor Carter H. Harrison, who had come to ring the New Liberty Bell. After the beer-wagon delay, he experienced more difficulties getting to the Bell: 75,000 people surrounded it, and those from out of town did not recognize Chicago's mayor. But when his identity was made known, he quickly passed through the crowd.

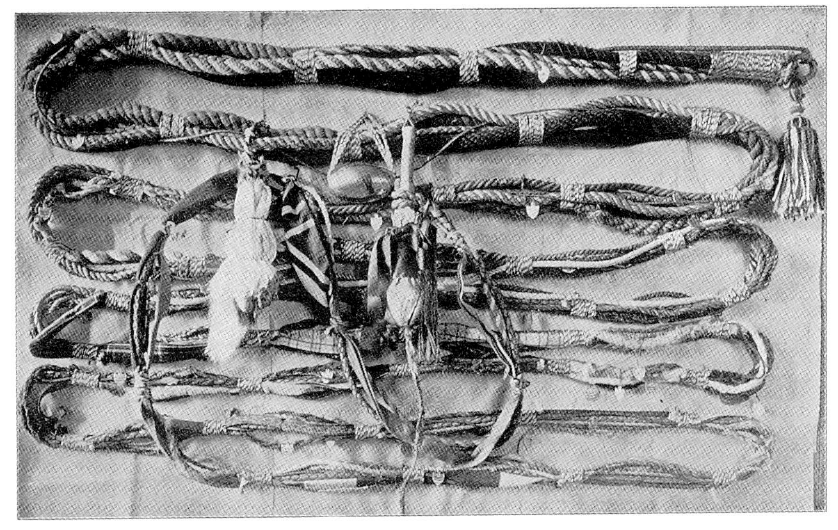
The International Rope Made for Chicago Day

The ringing of the Bell not only celebrated Chicago Day but also recognized the anniversary of the cession to the United States of the land on which Chicago stands. Before he rang the Bell, Harrison received the original 1833 treaty signed by the father of Pottawatomie Chief Simon Pokagon that represented the transfer of 994,000 acres. He also was handed the ponderous international rope with which to ring the Bell, and he quickly reeled off 13 strokes for the original 13 states. This was the first use of the international rope, to be formally dedicated at 5 p.m.

The birch-bark-wrapped deed to the land and a copy of Chief Pokagon's message from the Indians were presented to Mayor Harrison by Emma C. Sickles. She said the authenticity of the treaty was corroborated by a copy, the heirloom of the son of a witness to the signing. The Mayor then spoke:

> Grateful to the spirits of the past, I am happy to receive this gift free from the hand of one worthy to bestow it. [Cheers.] Chicago is proving that it recognizes the benefits conferred through the treaty. I receive this from an Indian all the more grateful because in my own veins there courses the blood of an Indian. Before the days of Pokagon I had my origin in the blood that ran through Pocahontas. I stand here as an evidence that the Indian is worth something in this world. Now that I have the deed I will not prove to be a mean Indian giver and return it.

Fellow citizens, this is the proudest day I have ever had. [Cheers.] Chicago is determined to lead the world. I trembled for fear this would not be a good day, but I knew last night that God was on the side of Chicago. [Applause.] This great city arose from fire, and what it has accomplished speaks in the buildings on these grounds. [Applause.] What we see around us here proclaims Chicago the center of the United States, and, aye, the world. I was afraid I couldn't get in here, but the ladies kindly moved aside, and I was not permitted to kiss any of them. May Chicago's day prove the proudest in the record of all exposition. I thank you. [Cheers.]

Chief Pokagon was then joined by John Young, decked in war paint and eagle feathers, in a double ringing of the Liberty Bell. Young's Indian father was said to have named "Chicag," which was interpreted "where the skunk dwells."* With a voice so feeble his words had to be repeated by another to be heard, Pokagon spoke his message:

Chief Pokagon

Through the untiring efforts of a few friends of another race, I greet you. If any of you, my countrymen, feel the sting of neglect because your rights have been ignored in taking part in the world's great fair until now, I beseech you to lay aside all bitterness of spirit, and with hearts so pure and good, that these noble mothers and daughters that have so labored in our behalf for this, may rejoice that the kind seeds that they have sown have not fallen on dry and barren ground.

Let us not crucify ourselves by going over the bloody trails we have trod in other days; but rather let us look up and rejoice in thankfulness in the present; for out of the storm cloud of darkness that is around about us we now see helping hands stretched out to aid and strengthen us; while above the roar and crash of the cyclone of civilization are heard many voices demanding that no more agents, through party influence, shall be appointed to deal with us; demanding that places now filled with Indian agents incompetent for the trust shall be supplied by good and competent men; demanding that no more fire-water, the "beverage of hell," shall be sold or given to our people at home or abroad; demanding in words not misunderstood that we must lay aside all tribal relations and become citizens, kings and queens, of this great republic.

The question comes up to us again and again, 'What can be done for the best good of the remnant of our race?' The answer to me is plain and clear, and it matters not how distasteful it may seem to us. We must give up the pursuits of our fathers; however dear we may love the chase, we must give it up; we must teach our children to give up the bow and arrow that is born in their hearts; and in place of the gun we must take the plow and live as white men do; they are all around about our homes; the game is gone never to return, hence it is vain to talk about support from game and fish. Many of our people are now successful in raising grain and stock, and what they have done we all can do. Our children must learn that they owe allegiance to no clan or power on earth except these United States. They must learn and love to wave the stars and stripes and at all times to rejoice that they are American citizens.

Our children must be educated and learn the different trades of the white man. Thanks to the Great Spirit, this government has already established a few schools for that purpose and to learn of their success you have but to visit the Indian schools on these grounds, examine the work of the children, see the different articles they have made, examine their writing-books, and you will be convinced that they will be able to compete with the dominant race.

I was pained to learn that some who should have been interested in our people discouraged our coming to the fair, claiming openly that we are heartless, soulless, and Godless. Now let us all as one pray to the Great Spirit that he will open the eyes of their understanding and teach them to know that we are human as well as they. Touch them to know that:

Within the recess of the native's soul
There is a secret place, which God doth hold;
And though the storms of life do war around,
Yet still within, his image is found.

* Alternately named Chi-ca-gou—"the Place of the Wild Onion."

I am getting to be an old man. I often feel that one foot is uplifted to step into the world beyond, but I am thankful that the measure of my days have been lengthened out, and that I am able to stand before you in this great congress for our people, in this the 400th year of the white man's advent in our father's land. In my infancy I was taught to love my chief and tribe, but since then the Great West has been swallowed up by the white man, and by adoption we are the children of this great republic. Hence we must teach loyalty to this nation, to our children, and solemnly impress upon them that the war path leads but to the grave.

I shall cherish as long as I live the cheering words that have been spoken to me here by ladies, friends of my race; it has strengthened and encouraged me; I have greater faith in the success of the remaining few of my people than ever before. I now realize the hand of the Great Spirit is open in our behalf; already he has thrown his great search light upon the vault of heaven, and Christian men and women are reading there in characters of fire well understood; 'The red man is your brother, and God is the father of all.'

One of the ladies Chief Pokagon was referring to was Emma Sickles. She had written about unfair treatment of the Indians by the "Friends of the Indian" movement, which took Indian youth from their parents and placed them in eastern Indian schools. She also had taken exception to the Indian General Allotment Act of 1887 (Dawes Act).

Festival Hall Morning Program

At 11:30 a.m. in Festival Hall, the Russian Choir of 30 voices, directed by Madame Eugenie Lineff, gave a performance of a Russian peasant wedding. An attendee thought that if the wedding was representative, it must be dreary in Russia. Almost before the Hall was cleared, Frank Taft followed with an organ recital of patriotic music. The *Herald* felt he had "too much Taft on his programme."

The Bands

Sharing the attention of the shifting crowd, six bands played a series of continuous elaborate concerts around the grounds: The Elgin Band conducted by J. Hecker; Chicago Band, Adolph Liesegang; Cincinnati Band, Michael Brand; Iowa State Band, Frederick Phinney; The Eighth Cavalry Band from Mexico, Encarnacion Payen; and the Pullman Band, J. F. Hostrawser.

The Elgin Band had possession of Wooded Island where it was scheduled to give concerts from 10 a.m. to noon, 2 to 4 p.m., and 6 to 9 p.m. It also preceded the Chicago Hussars in the morning parade, and due to delays, probably arrived late on Wooded Island.

The Elgin Band at the World's Columbian Exposition

The 50-piece Chicago Band played at the north bandstand from 6 to 9 p.m. Immediately after Chicago Day, this band was dismissed from employment at the world's fair, because its members, who belonged to the Chicago Musical Society, refused to play with the Cincinnati Band which would not join the union.

In addition to accompanying the Columbian Chorus outdoors in the morning and at Festival Hall at 4 p.m., the Cincinnati Band played at the Music Pavilion on the lakefront in mid-afternoon and again from 7 to 9 p.m. They had been hired for the entire six months of the fair by Theodore Thomas, orchestral director and predecessor of W. L. Tomlins.

The Iowa State Band was to play at the lakefront pavilion from 10 a.m. to noon. However, if it got there, the band was late, because it had led off the morning musical program at Terminal Plaza, which did not start until the belated hour of 11 a.m. They also led the "Reunion of States" at 2 p.m.

The location of most of the Mexican Band's performances was not recorded in the newspapers, but there was mention that it had become a popular band among Chicagoans, and its performances were well received. During the evening fireworks, it played from a balcony of Administration to a crowd which had gathered in the rotunda.

The Mexican Band at the World's Columbian Exposition

Starting early in the morning, the Pullman Band played at intervals and then continuously from 2 to 5 p.m. on the south side of the Illinois Building where the grounds and promenades were filled with appreciative auditors. From 5 to 7 p.m., it played at the lakefront.

The Hussars Exhibition Drill

The Chicago Hussars exhibition drill was to have taken place at 11 a.m. in the Stock Pavilion, with Captain Edwin L. Brand commanding. They were to have left their armory and proceeded by way of Michigan and Grand Avenues to be at the west gate of Midway Plaisance at 10 o'clock. Because of crowds encountered outside Jackson Park, their planned brisk trot was reduced to a slow step with badly broken ranks. It was nearly 11 a.m. when the Hussars entered the Midway Plaisance gate. The 50-piece Elgin Band was waiting inside to precede the staff officers, trumpeter corps, and Hussars—four abreast—down the Midway while playing a stirring march to which the spirited black horses were to prance in perfect time. The Hussars wore dark-blue uniforms slashed with silver and helmets with white flowing horsehair plumes. Their drawn sabers flashed in the sunlight as they formed into platoon files to proceed east down Midway Plaisance. The multitude crowded the entire roadway, so they came to a dead stop. It was not until the police were placed in the lead that some progress was made through the crowd. As the Hussars passed, the Midway crowd clapped and shouted enthusiastically. Step by step, the big band ahead, the elite troop proceeded in platoon front-of-eight toward the east. At the Woman's Building the procession wheeled left and in a circuitous route passed in front of the state buildings, marched around Manufactures and Administration, where they tangled with the crowd listening to the musical program, and finally entered the Stock Pavilion. The journey from the gate had taken one and one-half hours!

The Hussars Moving South Past Administration Through the Chicago Day Crowd Gathered for Music and Liberty Bell Activities

Twenty to twenty-five thousand people were waiting for the Hussars in the great open-air amphitheater of the Stock Pavilion. It was filled from the topmost ridge down into the arena and out through its four entrances. Of the crowd, about 8000 were children; and prior to the arrival of the Hussars, they overran the place.

Loudly announcing the Hussars arrival was a trumpeter riding a coal-black charger. He was followed into the amphitheater by the Elgin Band and, finally, the Hussars. A lively tune was started; the troops lined up for orders. The captain's saber flashed in the air, giving the signal "Forward."

The exhibition drill is technically known as the school of the troops. First, the magnificent horses walked around the ring; then, suddenly, there was a sharp order, and away the troopers went at a trot. The *Tribune* described what followed: "Around the ring once, then again, then the bugler gave the signal to gallop, from a gallop came the charge, first in twos, next threes, fours, finally down the arena twelve horses deep. Then came the cheering again. Cheer on cheer greeted the wheeling of the horses at the corners as they settled from the charge to the gallop, back to the trot, then the walk, and finally at a dead stand at the order 'Halt!'" The drill lasted about 40 minutes; and when it was over, the delighted crowd gave the Hussars a thunderous ovation.

Nearly all those who were in the audience had brought lunch baskets and, by staying to eat lunch in the amphitheater, avoided crowding at the exits.

Reunion of States Parade, Illustrated by Youths and Maidens

Promptly at 2 p.m., the parade started at the Court of Honor; but long before that time, the broad ways bounding the Court were gorged with people. The crowding was so dense that movement seemed impossible. Great white statues along the waterways were black with those who had climbed up and held tight to their stations despite protestations of the Columbian Guard. Hoping to have a vantage point, other people stood, sat, and hung from windows, ledges, balconies, and roofs.

This expectant waiting crowd gave a mighty shout as the procession, preceded by a platoon of Columbian guards and the Iowa State Band, entered the Court of Honor from the south end of the Peristyle and wound its way along the south facade of Manufactures. It seemed impossible that a way could be cleared through the dense throng; but as the procession approached, a path cleared in some unaccountable way, leaving a lee in front at all times of only a few yards.

Municipal Seal

Following the Iowa State Band came an honor guard of 34 youths representing Chicago—one child for each ward of the city. They bore shields on which the municipal seal was emblazoned and in large letters was the single word "Welcome." Children typified an embryonic Chicago and the promise of future generations.

Next came 100 boys of the Diocesan Choir carrying banners and representing the gift of song. The director had intended that they sing the patriotic hymn "Love and Liberty," which had been specially written for the day; but shouts of the noisy crowd quashed their attempts. The boys' choir was followed by the Ninth Presbyterian Cadets.

It was an ambitious parade, and by far, the grandest part was the five-section Reunion of States which followed the Cadets. Over 3000 girls and boys from Chicago took part. Entering earlier at the Sixty-second Street gate, the children had rendezvoused back of the Agricultural Building. They had arrived on the grounds dressed as the characters they were to represent and were a zestful kaleidoscope of color, freshness, and beauty.

For the first section, representing the 13 original states, girls in snowy white costumes marched, each wearing a gold crown with a star. They carried aloft banners and bore shields of those states; they also carried olive branches and various other emblematic state tokens. Even though it was eleventh of the original states to ratify the constitution, as an appeasement for losing the bid to host the world's fair, New York was at the head of the column in the post of honor.

Another reminder of American history came next: Twenty-four boys, in continental uniforms, marched proudly behind the original states. They represented the best of the First Regiment of Illinois (Chicago) Cadets. The *Herald* said, "Their quaint uniforms caused mingled wonder and amusement."

Of the 44 states in 1893, the remaining 31 were divided into the next four sections, appearing for the most part in the order in which they were admitted to the Union. Before every state came the coat of arms borne by a girl or boy representing the principal city in that state. Each state was allowed one representative for each of its counties and six to typify its six principal cities. While laurel and olive branches were borne by a large percentage of representative counties, in many cases the typical flower or even a cereal of the state was used instead.

Proudly leading the second section was the Stonewall Brigade Band from Stanton, Virginia. The band had tooted for Stonewall Jackson thirty years before when he led a brigade across the tobacco fields of Virginia; they were present when General Robert E. Lee surrendered; they had kept up their organization after the war and played at former President Ulysses S. Grant's funeral and President Grover Cleveland's inauguration.

The first state in the second section was Vermont, admitted in 1791 and represented by 14 girls for its 14 counties. The other states in this section followed in this order: Kentucky in 1792 with 117 counties; Tennessee in 1796 with 96 counties; Ohio in 1803 with 88 counties and represented by buckeyes; Louisiana in 1812 with 52 counties, represented by stalks of sugar cane and cotton bolls; Indiana in 1816 with 92 counties, represented by wheat and great stalks of corn; and Mississippi in 1817 with 75 counties. Most of the girls in this section were dressed in simple white gowns with silken sashes and crowns bearing a single gilt star; they carried shields bearing the name of the state and county represented. The boys wore white caps with red, white, and blue bands.

The third section was led by Illinois, admitted in 1818 with 102 counties. The beautiful banner of blue with the single word "Chicago" led Illinois' principal cities and called forth more cheers than any other emblem in the parade. Also carried by the children representing Illinois were portrait banners of General John A. Logan, President Abraham Lincoln, and Black Eagle. Illinois was followed by: Alabama in 1819 with 76 counties and represented by heads of wheat and cotton bolls tucked around its banners; Maine in 1820 with 16 counties had pine trees depicted on its banners; Missouri in 1821 with 115 counties had heads of wheat in the liberty caps of the boys and girls who marched for her; Arkansas in 1836 with 76 counties had banners of cotton bolls and sugar cane; Michigan in 1837 with 85 counties displayed wheat sheaves and apples; and for Florida in 1845 with 45 counties, every girl and boy carried apples, oranges, and other fruit. The children in this division wore liberty caps of red with upturned star-studded crowns of blue.

The fourth section was headed by Texas which was admitted in 1845 with 212 counties. Texas was followed in order by: Iowa in 1846 with 90 counties, represented by sheaves of wheat; Wisconsin in 1848 with 68 counties; California in 1850 with 54 counties, represented by gilded stalks of corn; Minnesota in 1858 with 80 counties; and Oregon in 1859 with 31 counties.

Admitted in 1861, Kansas' 102 representatives each bearing great stalks of corn headed the fifth section. Then followed: West Virginia in 1863 with 54 counties, Nevada in 1864 with 14 counties, Nebraska in 1867 with 92 counties, Colorado in 1876 with 55 counties, Washington in 1889 with 34 counties, Montana in 1889 with 17 counties, North Dakota in 1889 with 54 counties, and, finally, South Dakota in 1889 with 77 counties. Idaho and Wyoming, both admitted in 1890, were not mentioned.

Angling slowly through the crowd, this great slash of parade color crawled through the tiers of onlookers. For those who could see the procession, the scene was inspiring; for the rest, it was a major disappointment. Once wedged in between the lines of people, the children were so completely swallowed up that 20 feet away from the procession only the very tops of their numerous banners and gonfalons were visible. The parade completely encircled the Court of Honor, but planned evolutions at the Peristyle proved impracticable and were omitted from the program.

Game of Lacrosse and "Sampson"

In mid-afternoon at the Stock Pavilion amphitheater, Iroquois and Pottawatomie Indians whose fathers and grandfathers had taken part in the history of early Illinois and Chicago were pitted against one another in a game of lacrosse. Nearly all the seats were filled. The Indians were covered with many colors of paint, old eagle feathers, and bear cloths. Chief Pokagon was the honorary umpire and occupied a seat in the press box. Newspaper comments included the terms "savage," "mass of red faces and scant clothing," and "the fun of watching twenty Indians in a heap." At the end of the game, the Iroquois were declared the winner and remained on the field surrounded by several thousand curious people, who evidently had never seen an Indian before. The *Herald* called it a burlesque game—"lacrosse as it should not be played."

Sharing billing with the lacrosse game was "Sampson"—a strong man whose show provided great amusement for the children, who made up the majority of the audience. When he appeared in the ring, arrayed in his yellow tights with silver bangles, the children started cheering; and they kept it up until the end of his performance. Among other feats of strength, he upheld ten Columbian guards who stood on a plank that rested on his chest. Adults had to pay 50 cents to see the Indian lacrosse game and Sampson, but children were admitted free. With the exception of Sampson, the afternoon show was a failure; and disappointed patrons left feeling they had wasted both time and money.

Balloon Ascension

Between 3 and 4 p.m., at Government Plaza, aeronaut Samuel Baldwin of Quincy, Illinois, ascended in a hydrogen-filled balloon. This was ascension number 387, and he had never before flown in the presence of a crowd half this size. Baldwin's trip is described in the next chapter.

Festival Hall Afternoon Musical Program

At 4 p.m. in Festival Hall, the Chicago Columbian Chorus again assembled under the direction of Mr. Tomlins; and a part of the morning program was repeated. This time, organist Louis Falk accompanied Brand's Cincinnati Band in patriotic tunes, songs of home, and international airs. Voices were heard much better in the hall than they had been in the open air. Again, the concert ended with "America"; and people left with spirits uplifted.

International Rope Ceremonies

Boom! Boom! Boom! At 5 p.m. the New Liberty Bell was rung again, announcing the international ceremonies. This time it was rung in honor of the nations and societies represented at the World's Columbian Exposition that had contributed to the international rope. The basis of the rope was rawhide manufactured in Chicago. Around the rawhide was entwined a conglomerate cord of many pieces, including flax woven by England's Queen Victoria. The handle was made of material that had fallen near Canyon Diablo* in a meteoric shower. The representatives tapped the Bell in the order in which their contribution had been received by the chairman: Great Britain, Russia, Spain, Denmark, Belgium, China, Switzerland, Australia, New Netherlands, Ontario, Algeria, Sweden, British Guiana, Jamaica, Siam, Ireland, Bombay, Norway, South Sea Islands, Monaco, France, Persia, Mexico, Manitoba, Liberia, Johore, Hawaii, Scotland, Guatemala, Alaska, Paraguay, Ceylon, Navajo Indians, The Red Cross Society, St. John's Association, Cape of Good Hope, New South Wales, Iroquois Indians, Orange Free States, Japan, Egypt, Brazil, Argentine Republic, Trinidad, Puerto Rico, Corea, Iceland, and Turkey.

The 5 p.m. Ringing of the New Liberty Bell With the International Rope, Chicago Day (Terminal Station in the Background)

The Night Pageant: "Chicago and Her Growth Welcoming the World"

The Floats. The floats had been stored in the Columbian Stables at Fifty-sixth Street and East End Avenue. An unfinished clubhouse next to the stables was turned into a dressing room for the women who rode on them as allegorical and historical figures. By 5 p.m. such a large crowd had congregated about the stable doors that police had to drive it back. To reach the fairgrounds from the stables, the celebration committee brought the floats west on Fifty-sixth Street to Stony Island Avenue, then south over the Midway Plaisance viaduct to the Sixty-second Street gate—seven blocks total. An immense crowd had gathered along the route from the stable to the gate to watch the progress. When the order was given to start, the Irish floats had not appeared; and the procession began without them.

---

* Discovered in 1891, it is also known as Meteor Crater and is located 19 miles west of Winslow, Arizona.

East Plaza of the Administration Building. Gathering for the Night Pageant, Chicago Day.

Meanwhile, preparations for the arrival of the floats were taking place within the fairgrounds. Ropes had been strung along the line of march with a passage 15 feet wide. People staked out their viewing positions, grabbed the ropes and, though jostled from behind, would not budge during their two-hour wait for the parade to begin. Just inside the gate in a small space between the Service Building and the fence, an unbelievable 3000 managed to squeeze.

Gathering for the Night Pageant

Within the gates, the entire line of march was soon walled with expectant viewers. The Administration Building was the center of the maelstrom; people filled the rotundas, crowded the ledges, leaned out on poles, and banked themselves against the building. Boaters had arrived by one of three entrances from Lake Michigan—north inlet, south inlet, or water gate; and 50,000 excited people in gondolas, canoes, dug-outs, electric launches, catamarans, and steam yachts awaited the pageant.

At 6:30 p.m. the great parade of floats was poised to enter the Sixty-second Street gate; those inside could hear the crowd outside cheering. Abruptly, the gate opened; and the Chicago Hussars, their white plumes streaming, swept through. Captain E. L. Brand, marshal of the Night Pageant, was in the lead. The Columbian Guard lost control over the crowd, and suddenly the ropes which had been stretched along the line of march were beaten down. The people stood face to face with the horsemen.

Finally, a narrow way was cleared, and behind the Hussars came the first float, "The Genius of Music." Drawn by magnificently matched horses and illuminated by the steady glare of calcium lights, it was "one of the prettiest floats" in the procession. A woman robed in white and gold stood in the center of the float and played a harp. Around her were grouped 50 singing women; but the cheering was wild, and their song was lost in the babel of the crowd.

The Hussars Leading the Night Parade — East of the Manufactures Building Going North

People pushing to get a glimpse of the next float were shoved back as the eight black horses pulling "Chicago 'I Will'" appeared at the gate. The focus of the float was "I Will"—Miss E. Flynn—wearing robes of white and gold, standing on a globe with outstretched arms, and welcoming all peoples of the world. On the panels which supported her were emblazoned in golden scrolls the dates memorable in the history of Chicago. The support was surrounded by 44 young girls, each holding a shield and representing a state. Robed women representing music, art, science, and literature stood on pedestals at the four corners of the float and shone beautifully in the dazzling limelight.

Second Float: "Chicago 'I Will'"

The third float, drawn by 16 roan horses, was entitled "Chicago in 1812." Representing the birth of Chicago, it depicted several things: On top of a large pedestal, a friendly Indian was saving a white woman—a Fort Dearborn soldier's wife—from certain death under the tomahawk of a "savage Indian"; on either side of the pedestal appeared drawings of old Fort Dearborn and the hut of John Kinzie, first white settler in Chicago. Below the base, other Indian groups sat, including a trio of Cherokee girls singing the songs of their tribe and Chief Pokagon holding the original deed. In the rear, a robed Catholic friar and buckskin-clad frontiersman spoke with an Indian. This float was sponsored by the Iroquois Club. "Buffalo Bill's

Third Float: "Chicago in 1812"

"Chicago 'I Will'" During the Parade by Herbert E. Butler (*Harper's Weekly*)

Wild West" show loaned 14 Indians and a scout. Writing for the *Daily News*, Amy Leslie, who later authored *Amy Leslie at the Fair*, reported that all requests of Cody were met with ready patriotism even when he was decidedly inconvenienced.

Torchbearers, wearing gilded helmets and white capes, ran alongside "Chicago in 1812" and the next float, "Chicago at War." The big teams were cared for by men dressed in all the panoply of green, brown, and gold.

To celebrate the proud part Chicago and the State of Illinois had played in the Civil War, the Sheridan Club's float, "Chicago in War," portrayed General Philip Sheridan out front on his gray charger riding to victory at Winchester, Grant and Logan on pedestals behind him, followed by Stephen A. Douglas and Richard Yates. Above them President Lincoln held the Emancipation Proclamation, and just above him, Chicago "I Will" held out her arms to offer these, her sons, on the altar of liberty. The leading characters were members of the Sheridan Club. At the back of the float was a group of Chicago Zouaves, portrayed by surviving Civil War Veterans, with a man representing Colonel Elmer E. Ellsworth leading them in a charge. Carved on the panels of the float were the names of Chicago men who had died in war.

Fourth Float: "Chicago in War"

At 7 o'clock the electric lights on the Administration dome and on the cornices above the Plaza and the Court of Honor were extinguished. Only the torches on Administration blazed, and the crown over the dome stood out against the deep blue sky. The flags were hauled down from the flagstaffs all about the grounds. The north corridor of

Machinery Hall had been reserved for the council committee and their invited guests. Here, Governor Altgeld and his staff in full uniform, the mayor, and city officials watched the pageant.

The first float passed in front of the Administration Building at 7:30 p.m. After the fourth float passed that point, confusion ensued. Several of the subsequent floats could not pass beneath the Intramural Road trestle at the Sixty-second Street entrance and had to detour. Many in the crowd at the Court of Honor left their advantageous places and hurried to the lakefront where the fireworks had just started. The break in the pageant lasted about an hour; and when the cry reached the multitude at the Peristyle that floats were reappearing, they rushed back; but the crowd that saw the rest of the parade from the Court of Honor was not nearly as large as the patient group that had previously waited so long.

Six matched and glistening white horses drew the fifth float: "Chicago in Peace." On the high central pedestal was a chariot drawn by cupids and driven by an angel of peace holding a laurel wreath high in the air. It was a float of many colors; pale blue and pink shaded into crimson and deepened into black. The cupids, the only non-living figures, were twined with flowers and blew silver trumpets. Pictured on panels below the chariot were homes of modern cliff dwellers and commerce towers. Four women sat on the corners and represented the four chief industries which paid tribute to Chicago: building, textile manufacturers, agriculture, and iron manufacturers.

Next came "Chicago Prostrate," depicting the devastating fire of 1871. A large figure—"The Fire Fiend"—carrying a huge torch looked down on the rubble of the prostrate city. At his feet crouched a mother holding two trembling babies in her arms. Through the smoke, the crowd could see a fireman carry a child from a burning building. The colors were appropriately red, yellow, and black; but some thought the float lacked in red light and a lurid glow that would accompany a blaze. The

Waiting Around the Basin for the Night Pageant

Fifth Float: "Chicago in Peace"

Sixth Float: "Chicago Prostrate" or "The Fire Fiend"

float, pulled by six of the fire department's great horses, was manned by veteran Chicago firemen of 1871 still employed in 1893.

After the fire float, there was a another delay: 20 minutes at the entrance gate. Further along the line, people who had been standing immobile in crushing conditions for several hours grew disgusted and started to fill in the gap behind the floats already in the Court of Honor.

Then came the old fire engine that had done duty in the fire of 1871—Old Economy No. 9. The cheering crowd went wild when they saw the relic. It had been polished, covered with flags and flowers, and was drawn by a trusty team. There was confusion along the parade route; and at some point, the old fire engine apparently overtook the fire float.

The seventh float, "Commerce," furnished by the Chicago Board of Trade, was represented by an argosy glittering entirely in gold and white and flaunting a single sail. The mast was draped with flowers and topped with a gay banner. A woman representing commerce sat high on a seat, which was supported on four iron wheels like those of a locomotive. The "Three Graces" offered her fruit and flowers. On either side huge cornucopias emptied their wealth of plenty, while at the rear "Good Fortune" sat, steering the ship of Chicago's progress. The lower part of the float was the ocean from which mermaids rose at the four corners lifting their offerings from the cardinal points. About the sides of the float and up the mast and yardarm ran a blaze of electrical lights that looked like pearls; and at the head of each of the eighteen horses, three abreast, that pulled this float, glowed electric lights in red, white, and blue. The horses were led by grooms in gold-trimmed white coats and white hats.

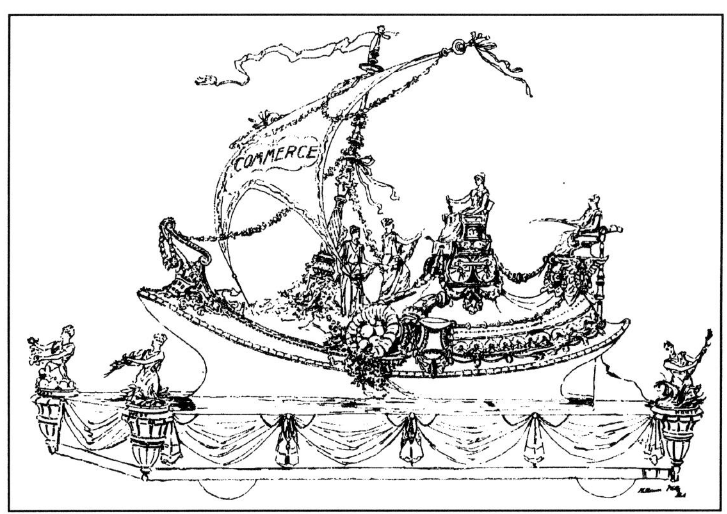

Seventh Float: "Commerce"

People went wild over the beauty of "Commerce," and yet it was this float that caused such a delay in the procession. After it had entered the grounds, the sail was hoisted, and the engines readied for lighting the strings of lights. The work took half an hour. The first few floats had almost doubled back on the parade route before "Commerce" was ready. But once it took off and rounded Festival Hall, it was a grand success.

The Columbus Club sponsored the eighth and last float in the first set: "Columbus at the Court of Isabella." It literally dashed through the gate and was "the most spectacular of all." Celebrating the moment that made the World's Columbian Exposition possible, the humble sailor, Columbus, bowed to Spain's Queen Isabella and King Ferdinand. Covered with gems, their thrones had a magnificent canopy of purple silk which was supported by four golden standards. To one side with attendant monks stood the scarlet-robed Cardinal Televera, who gazed at a globe and contemplated the navigator's plan. The Queen was dressed in gold and white robes. Rich Oriental rugs and tapestry hung over all the float, and orange blankets bearing the royal

Eighth Float: "Columbus at the Court of Isabella"

arms of Castile and Aragon were draped over the six black horses which pulled it.

After all of the first set of floats had passed around Manufactures into the lakefront area, the crowd pushed north after them. During the lull before the second section came in sight, many moved south and west around the corner of Manufactures where they met and fought with the crowds from the Peristyle area. Scratches, bruises, and crushing injuries were numerous. Ambulances could not get through. The crowd was so dense it was practically impossible for benevolent men to carry out the fainting women. Children were crying from twisted and sprained arms and legs. Men cursed and fought to protect the women and children, and failing, gave up in despair.

Then followed the second set of floats; these were furnished by foreign-born residents of Chicago. Many were accompanied by cavalcades with riders in historical costumes.

The fireworks had already begun. Showers of red and green stars illuminated the sky east of Manufactures. Many groans were heard from people who would have liked to see the pyrotechnic display but found they could not move in the crowd. Searchlights, mounted on Manufactures, swept around the park, occasionally illuminating the floats. And rockets seemed to drop their stars on the floats as they rounded Festival Hall.

The British float, "The Early Discoveries and First Settlers," was a large single-masted boat. On a raised platform in the center stood "John Cabot" with a globe. Positioned around the deck were figures representing Sir Walter Raleigh, Sir Francis Drake, some Puritans, Captain John Smith, and Pocahontas. Members of societies of Englishmen in Chicago played the character parts. The float was drawn by 12 horses.

Great Britain

Swedish-Americans chose to bring to life the ancient legend: "The Vikings and Valkyries in Valhalla." Drawn by 12 horses, each carrying a woman in the costume of a Valkyrie and led by a Viking, the gorgeous float itself was the site of great merrymaking as the feast of Valhalla took place. Thor presided over other gods of Norse legend, and a male chorus sang Swedish folk songs.

Sweden

German-Americans entered two floats. "Germany in Art, Science and Industry" was depicted by a central triumphal arch with Germania on the keystone; and in the arch were Johann Gutenberg, Johann Faust, Johannes Kepler, Johann Wolfgang von Göethe, Alexander von Humboldt, Johann Sebastian Bach, Immanuel Kant, Justus von Liebig, and Johann Schiller. The Goddess of Liberty stood in the center of the second float, "The German-Americans in the History of the U.S. 1776 and 1861," and was surrounded by a group of German figures important in the Revolutionary and Civil Wars.

Although the official program listed one float, Bohemia's contribution to the parade was variously described as one and two floats. Either way, their presentation was elaborate. Jan Hus, the religious reformer, figured prominently, as did allegorical figures representing art, science, industry, and agriculture, which paid homage to a central figure of Bohemia. Either preceding or between the two was a procession of peasants and peasant girls dressed in various national costumes who represented a new era for this country fighting to regain independence after the Thirty Years War.

The French-Canadians entered two floats. One represented the first boat that brought white men to the shores of Canada in 1534—"La Grande Hermine." The boat carried figures of explorer

Jacques Cartier, an Indian companion, and a boatman. A figure representing "Marquette Landing in Chicago, 1673" rode on the second float.

Bohemia

A reporter, whose description of the parade places him near the entrance gate, spoke of two Irish floats following the French-Canadians: "St. Brendan, the First Discoverer" and "The Genius of Erin." Reporters further down the line did not mention Ireland. Since we know the floats were delayed at the stable, this raises the question whether there actually were Irish floats in the parade. It is possible that, in all the confusion, the Irish floats were either extremely delayed or abandoned somewhere in the park.

Ireland

Denmark's contribution was its "Tappere Landsoldat," the national guard of that country.

Norwegian-Americans presented two floats. "Norway 1000 Years Ago" carried the figure of Leif Erickson in his Viking ship with shields hanging over the gunnels. On the second, "Norway at Present," figures of Columbia and Nora touched hands in a friendly greeting.

Scheduled to provide four floats, the Polish-Americans may have had four at the start of the parade; but only two are mentioned by reporters further down the line: "Sobieska" representing the rescue of Vienna from Turkish rule, and "Adoption of the Constitution of Poland, 1791" proclaiming Polish independence.

Another delay followed—this time for 40 minutes. The crowd just inside the gate thought the parade of floats was over and tried to move away from the ropes, but when they turned around and pushed, people were so tightly pressed together that it was impossible to move. One reporter said that people were so wedged in that the voice became the only active part of the body. Women screamed and men swore as the jam became painful. Suddenly, a man found that he could get out through the revolving exit gates; when others followed, some of the pressure was relieved.

Then one of the Hussars dashed out onto Stony Island Avenue and came back with the report that the "Elestra" was coming. The gates had been left open; and while the guards peered after the Hussar, the outside crowd made a dash into the grounds.

Lit by 2000 incandescent lamps, Elestra—the genius of electricity—was an enormous ornate dragon sponsored by the General Electric and Chicago Edison

The Edison and General Electric Float "Elestra"

companies. As planned, its writhing body changed color from green to red, its gaping mouth exhaled flaming breath, and there were dazzling lights along its flapping wings. It was the old monster of lightning and storm, conquered by man and harnessed to do his bidding in all the varied uses of electricity.

Extremely late, Elestra was lumbering its way from the stables and had gotten as far as Fifty-seventh Street. Going downhill, the float was just too heavy for its team of 12 horses. Ropes had to be procured and fastened to the rear so that 100 men could act as brakes as the float moved down the decline of the Midway Plaisance overpass. Over at the Court of Honor, Elestra did not make an appearance until at least 9 p.m., perhaps considerably later.

The *Herald* gave an account of the bisection of the procession and abandonment of some floats:

> Shortly after the procession entered the grounds the people crowded about the floats in the first section in such numbers as to delay the second section. As they advanced, the gap between the sections widened and was filled by the following throng. It was impossible to keep the people back or to close up the ranks of the procession, which became bisected, and some of the floats were at last actually swamped in the crowd east of the Manufactures Building on the lake front. The first section moved on as slowly as possible to give the others time to close the growing gap but it could not be done. Those who would have kept back were powerless to do so owing to the pressure from behind. The horses were unhitched from several of the floats, which were deserted and left standing where they were abandoned.

Without naming them, the *Tribune* reported that many floats built for Chicago Day were not used because the designer, William L. Wells, would not allow them to be used without the proper lights, and those the contractors had failed to secure.

It was spectacular. It was a mess. In spite of displays of temper at the Peristyle and the sorrows of the great delays between floats, the vast majority of the crowd was still in remarkably good spirits when it was over.

The Fireworks. Promptly on schedule at 8 p.m., a man pushed his way through the crowd, struck a match on overalls, lit a fuse, and the fireworks display began.* Twin crimson lines of light blazed north and south like flashes of red lightning. The massed thousands cheered and started in a steady current towards the lakefront to the east. Lost in the roar of the crowd was the music of half a dozen bands. From a dozen places about the grounds, 200 rockets and bombs hissed all over creation, filling the horizon with spangles of fire and color. A short while later, huge bombs of magnesium—500 pounds total—were ignited simultaneously on Wooded Island, at the Court of Honor, and on the lakefront; they lit up the entire White City; and in the dazzling light, electric lamps seemed dim. Several times colored rockets were fired from all three areas; and as the lights of the magnesium bombs faded, the heavens were again and again studded with new stars. The events at each site are described separately below.

Before the lights were lit on Wooded Island, it was almost deserted. Then the illumination began, and soon every foot of space was occupied by a human being. Trees were filled with 15,000 fairy lamps, outlining walks and flower gardens; there were red fires; Chinese lanterns cast a soft glow; bandstands were decorated; and bands played. Most of the watercraft carried colored lanterns, and the songs of the gondoliers wafted from the surrounding waters. Wooded Island had been transformed into a fairyland! When the fireworks began, people tramped through the flower beds to get a better view. When 27 little girls danced on a platform, the impatient crowd broke down barriers, trampled grass and flowers, and pressed so close to the platform that those in the rear could see nothing but bobbing heads. Fireworks consisted of double girandoles revolving horizontally; a 30- x 40-foot mosaic design containing lance work; aquatic novelty fireworks—dolphins, fairy fountains, flying fish, geysers, and torpedoes; a special fan device with 700 square feet of lance work with carved handles

---

* Described in the *Tribune* as originating at the west end of the Midway. No other accounts, including those in the *Tribune*, mentioned any fireworks displays on the Midway, which raises the question whether they were canceled there for safety reasons.

which represented a large ostrich; a mammoth silver fire wheel which cut a huge spray of fire, the same as the display in the Court of Honor; a battery of 500 meteors; a grove of jeweled palms surrounded by a sea of fiery spray; 50 floating fountains on the water around the island; a nest of 500 fiery cobras; and the finale—the illumination of Wooded Island with torches which changed color four times. When the activities were over, the *Herald* reported the crowd dispersed "as an impatient, tired, pushing, shouting, resistless mass that toiled up the inclines to the lagoon bridges, and, rushing pell-mell down the declines, was lost in the greater mass beyond."

The Court of Honor's broad avenues surrounding the Basin were filled with a teeming multitude. Chairs and benches were useless, and people were pressed forward against their will until they stood within the spray from the Electric and MacMonnies Fountains. Suddenly, ribbons of fire were stretched all about the Court; they fell down over the Grecian Peristyle. Fiery fish leaped from the water, and fountains spewed gold and crimson jets. Overhead a tight-rope walker traversed a trembling wire stretched between the Music Hall and the Casino. The 7:30 p.m. announcement that the lakefront fireworks could be viewed almost equally well from any point between Administration and the Peristyle had kept tens of thousands of people within the Court of Honor waiting for the show to begin. A second announcement that there would be special fireworks for the Court of Honor rivaling the brilliancy and extent of the lakefront displays did not prove to be quite true. Few noticed or cared. A mammoth silver fire wheel with six mutations went spinning, finishing as a revolving kaleidoscope. There was a rush and swish of explosive from a float in the central Basin of the Court. There was a screen of gold and silver. A flash, a report, and a hundred meteors blazed in the sky; another report, and 3000 Roman candles showered jewels. Another flash, and a grove of palms appeared. Masses of varicolored fires then burst near the fountains, illuminating them. A moment of darkness was followed by a beech tree with golden branches. Thousands of fiery serpents twisted in the water. The crowd was spellbound. "So constant was the noise and smoke," printed the *Herald*, "and so brilliant the flashing explosives in the central Basin, the crowd scarcely missed such set pieces as the great Niagara Falls, which was to have been given at the inner side of the Peristyle." Late on October 8, fair authorities served peremptory notice on F. D. Millet that there would be no fireworks within 200 feet of any building. This negated plans to fire set pieces in the Court of Honor, and the larger ones were moved to the lakefront. The resulting gaps in the program were filled with a multitude of smaller attractive displays. There was an intermittent reminder of ongoing events as a tardy float threaded its way through the throng, causing an occasional commotion at the edge of the crowd. A *Daily News* reporter commented that the fireworks display as seen from the west end of the Basin was fine but scarcely up to the expectations of the visitors. At times the view was badly obscured by the dense smoke from the powder ignited above the Lagoon.

Chicago Day Fireworks at the Court of Honor

At the lakefront, thousands of people had waited for hours. Many of them had secured their choice viewing spots by picnicking there in the afternoon. Other thousands poured in, and one mile of lakeshore 100 feet deep was a solid mass of one-quarter million people. East of Manufactures, between this ocean of people and the lake, was hung a gold chain to separate the people from the fireworks.

Suddenly, the lakefront was illuminated by 200 prismatic fires which changed color four times—a warning that the story to be told in lights was about to begin. Against the lakefront side of the Peristyle burned a 30- x 30-foot device which portrayed Chicago's first mayor, William B. Ogden, looking down on the crowd from "Old City Hall." A cheer arose in a glorious swell, and it was for Chicago. Then followed a 40- x 40-foot device on which was reproduced the log huts of old Fort Dearborn; they rose like a dim memory, and there were no cheers for the old fort. Next, out on the Lake, a 60- x 40-foot frame was lit showing a figure typifying the genius of Chicago; on one side rose the golden dome of Administration; and on the other, Manufactures; before them was an eagle with wings outstretched and talons sunk into the national coat of arms. These were the "Scenes of Former Days."

Stereoscopic View Card of the Chicago Day Illumination

In the interval between the above large devices and the burning of Chicago below, the men under pyro-technician Paine's direction on the lakefront set off an unbelievable twenty-five 24-inch bombs containing meteors; one hundred 15-inch bombs spraying jewels; fifty rockets each containing floating festoons of fire; twenty 30-inch shells with continuously changing novelties and effects; a depiction of Flora's bower produced by the discharge of one hundred 15-inch bombs fired by electricity; an entire lakefront illumination with three hundred floating lights of changing color; six double girandoles, extending 300 feet and discharging batteries, jewel mines rockets, and silver showers; a flight of fifty rockets with Paine's patented flash lights; twenty 36-inch shells spewing torrents of gold, pale green, silver and purple, amber, silver and lilac, mauve, turquoise, and crimson light; two hundred tourbillions raining overhead cones of fire; one hundred 15-inch bombs; one hundred rockets bearing continuously-changing festoons of fire; ten of Paine's mammoth 50-inch bombs containing 10,000 stars; one hundred 15-inch shells fired by electricity and forming a perfect aerial umbrella of every color of the rainbow; two hundred of Paine's aquatic novelties; five of Paine's mammoth 60-inch bombs, each weighing 100 pounds and containing 15,000 stars (the largest ever fired); fifty of Paine's liquid fire rockets; Paine's celebrated shell of shells; 1000 pounds of compound from the ends of Casino and North Piers, lighting up the sky and making one artistic blend of color clouds of new tints;

Chicago Day Search Arc Lights and Fireworks at the Court of Honor

two hundred fifty rockets forming a floating wheat sheaf; fifty whistling rockets; and twenty rockets of shimmering gold.

At this point, the *Tribune* described a 320- x 45-foot set device with a series of four pictures that began at the left and consisted of the Chicago River, the Light-House, the Lake Hotel, and the Rush Street Bridge; and it continued right into the description of Mrs. O'Leary's cow. The four-scene device was neither on the program nor mentioned in other papers.

Chicago Day Night Pageant by Charles Graham

The next set device depicted scenes from the Chicago fire of 1871. The frame's dimensions were a huge 300 x 50 feet. Mrs. O'Leary's cow appeared first, and the crowd cheered when her shape first showed against the sky; they cheered again when her name broke out in green lights on her side, and they shouted lustily when a lamp appeared behind her heels, which kicked wildly at the lamp. The *Herald*, thought it strange "that after all the trouble and misery caused by that cow, one of the biggest crowds that ever got together on American soil ... cheered that mischievous old cow's picture. And that crowd mainly composed of Chicagoans, too! And on Chicago's own day, of all days of the year!" Next was shown the panic on the quay; and while the frames dropped, red tongues of fire leaped up about the buildings—the conflagration was at its height. Suddenly, the Great Powder Company standing at one end of the frame exploded, and the picture vanished in smoke. One thousand pounds of explosives were used in this display. When it was over, a *Herald* reporter wrote: "Although this was only a sketch in the sky, the people looked as sober as if they were actually gazing on the scene of war from which a young Chicago sprang in glory!"

The *Tribune* reported that the Niagara Falls set piece took place earlier along the east side of the Peristyle and was ignited by Director-General Davis, who pressed an electric button in his office in Administration and then ran to the window and looked towards the display. The *Herald* account places Niagara as the last set piece. A Niagara of determination and grit, depicted in torrents of golden fire, it exemplified "Chicago Triumphant." When Niagara died, part of the crowd began to scatter. Thousands stayed to watch the finale—the flight of three hundred 15-inch bombs and a bouquet of 5000 rockets that filled the sky.

In its day, it was the greatest fireworks display ever and showed the results of Paine's hard work and inventiveness. But there was too much display for some, and perhaps part of it had a sameness which made the crowd restless. They wanted variety.

Thousands of people, weary of fireworks and processions, crowded into the rotunda of the Administration Building to be serenaded by Gianini, whose guitar and songs could be heard from the balcony leading to President Higinbotham's office. Dressed as a gondolier, he was accompanied by an Italian orchestra of guitars and mandolins. When he stopped between encores, the Mexican Band played from a balcony across the pavilion. The grateful crowd kept them singing and playing until the last of the skyrockets burst over the Peristyle.

"Old Glory" Balloon From July 4th Which Was Also Flown on Chicago Day

The story was nearing a close. Chicago's former days had been recounted. Chicago in ashes had been depicted. Chicago of the day had been shown. And finally, Chicago emerged triumphant, akin to Niagara Falls, one of the wonders of the world.

Across from the Court of Honor swelled strains of the "Star Spangled Banner." The music was the signal for the floating of the flag. Amid cheers, a monster balloon slowly rose and floated out over the black Lake; far below it hung, in fireworks display, the stars and stripes of "Old Glory."

Midnight saw the end. The heralds played a second fanfare, the lights blinked out, and the last of the crowd headed home. Chicago Day was over.

Leaving the Fair

Some fairgoers left as early as 4 p.m. to avoid the jam. Of those who stayed on for the evening's activities, many departed during the procession of floats; when the parade became bifurcated, thousands who saw the first section thought they had seen it all and headed for their trains.

Then, all those still in the park seemed to want to go home at once; and the great rush began in earnest. The result of so large a number of people trying to leave the grounds at once generated a terrific snarl at every transportation terminal in and near Jackson Park. And for hours, there was a solid knot of humanity around Transportation, Mines, and Terminal Station.

Elevated Railroad at the Transportation Building

The Alley "L" station inside the grounds at the Transportation Building was the site of the greatest crush. At 9 p.m. an estimated 30,000 tried to press through four exits that accommodated only two to three persons at a time. Thus, the solid mass of people had to melt into thin streams to pass through the narrow exits and up the stairs to the trains. As the crowd approached the exits, it gained momentum. Women screamed and children cried as they were pushed against the railings. Amid the crowd's shoving and struggling to get to the front and catch early trains, dresses were torn, hats lost, and friends separated. Only vigilant efforts by city police and Columbian guards, who mounted the sheds over the exits and pleaded with the crowd, prevented fatal accidents. Fairgoers obeyed the orders to stand back, although the effect of the pleading was lost on the fringes of the crowd where people—not quite so uncomfortable—jeered the guards.

An overwhelming amount of heat was generated by such a large group in close contact, and people began fainting. Those pressed against the boxes pleaded with the guards for assistance and were lifted up, then lowered on the other side of the sheds. Swooning women, young and old, were boosted up on the roofs where Dr. Gunn, the Alley "L" physician, and his assistants revived them. Many of the victims received the cold water treatment and walked away dazed and disheveled. Many more fainted to the floor and remained there waiting to be revived. Every minute there was a fresh victim. Many small children rode on their parents' shoulders; hundreds of others were passed up to guards on the roof to be kept safe until their parents could get through the gates and reclaim them. Frequent gongs were heard as ambulances tried to part the crowd to pick up victims. The wonder of it all is that nobody was more seriously hurt in the Alley "L" exodus.

Typical of newspapers around the country that gave graver accounts of the scene at Alley "L" station than those in Chicago, the *Janesville Gazette* reported that 150 men and women fainted, 40 women were taken away in the ambulance and patrol wagons, 4 died, and scores of people suffered terribly from the horrible jam. They described many more people, both men and women, being lifted to the roof of the shed: at one time, two rows of women were stretched lengthwise on the roof. They also spoke of a temporary hospital set up in the Transportation Building to which 40 women were carried.

The tremendous crowd at the Alley "L" station was augmented by people trying to make their way to the Sixty-fourth Street gates, losing their bearings, and becoming unwitting parties to the mayhem at Transportation. Once in the crowd, they could not get out.

Terminal Station

Although the biggest jam occurred at the Alley "L" in Transportation, by far the greatest number of people exited through Terminal Station. At 4 p.m. there were already a few passengers boarding the Illinois Central Express trains, at 5 p.m. every car had a moderate number, at 6 o'clock the trains were comfortably filled, and by 7 p.m. there was a current that swelled over the next hour and swamped the ticket sellers. The crowd stormed the gate, carrying along many people who could not give their tickets to collectors because they could not reach them. Out on the Plaza, people walked in comparative comfort, though their progress was slow; but once inside Terminal Station, they turned into a fighting mob. Women were pushed aside by stronger men, and children were crushed until they fainted. The crowd had to funnel between two rows of ticket booths; and many who were pushed through without tickets deposited their dimes, in lieu of tickets, in the boxes at the turnstiles. Others had a free ride. From 9 to 10 p.m., the crowd was at its worst. Columbian guards stationed there to preserve order were themselves swept through the gates and sometimes onto the trains. By 11:30 p.m. the remaining crowd could pass through the ticket booth area with little effort, and by midnight people rode downtown in comfort.

Fifty-seventh Street Gate

For three hours, the rush at the Fifty-seventh Street gate was also tremendous. Pressure here was relieved, because Superintendent Tucker had ordered the large wagon gates thrown open. People poured through the gates and over to the Illinois Central and the cable stations, as well as to several hundred vehicles stationed along the neighboring avenues for five to six blocks in every direction—everything from a swell four-in-hand to a rusty old lumber wagon with a hay rack. For a time it looked as if a great many people would spend the night waiting for some means of transportation, but the trains and vehicles moved them out rapidly. At one point it was estimated that 1000 people left the platforms of the Fifty-seventh Street station on the suburban trains every 20 minutes. The Fifty-seventh Street crowd also departed the fair by cable trains that left every minute packed with people and covered with others hanging on the footboards and riding on the roofs. The crowd rapidly dispersed. By 10:30 p.m. very few were still waiting, and the few thousand in the vicinity were people who had just come out of the fairgrounds.

Sixty-third Street

From 8:30 p.m. to midnight, the Sixty-third Street Illinois Central station was a mass of people. Train officials warned the patrons not to rush up on the platform because it was already packed enough for four train loads. The platform was about 12 feet in the air; including the space on the steps, it was designed to hold approximately 6000. Overloaded, around 9 p.m. an ominous cracking sound was heard in the heavy girders supporting the platform. Initially, the crowd obeyed orders to stand back but soon returned to occupy every available space. Trains were quickly filled and sent on their way.

The cross-town electric cars on Sixty-third Street were swamped. Some people, weary of awaiting elevated trains above, climbed down the supports and took positions on top of the electric cars; those leaving between 8:30 and 10:30 p.m. had their roofs completely covered with passengers. Only one accident was reported on this line: A car slipped back a few feet while ascending a slight grade and crashed into an express wagon loaded with people. One of the horses was killed, but no one in the wagon was injured.

An alternate means of egress was also found: At points from Sixty-third to Sixty-seventh Street, the crowd discovered holes in the fences and broke through in a continuous stream.

Madison Avenue Elevated

The greatest delays were experienced at the Elevated station on Madison Avenue just outside the grounds. Trains leaving from inside the grounds normally did not stop at this station, and only a few trains were made up and sent especially to this point. The stairs leading up to the ticket booths were gorged with people, and a line reaching 100 feet back from the stair entrance grew longer as time passed. Those on the stairs were prisoners for hours, since they could neither get to the depot nor return to the street.

Casino Pier

The first sizable homeward-bound load of steamboat passengers—3500—left Casino Pier at 9:15 p.m. To that time vessels had been transporting 50 to 100 persons a trip away from the park. When the big whaleback *Columbus* arrived at 9:45 p.m., such a throng was waiting on the pier it almost swept the ticket choppers and gatemen before it. At the close of Chicago Day, it was determined that the steamboats could have carried more passengers, but many fairgoers did not appreciate—or even think of—the Lake as a means of transportation. When the pageant was over, most of the crowd turned to the west to take the Elevated or Illinois Central.

Midway Plaisance Gates

Of those walking to cars via the Midway Plaisance after the fireworks, many dropped out of the procession before reaching the end of the street. Some fell asleep on benches; some went into side shows or stopped to eat and drink in pavilions and villages, which did a brisk business. As they waited for a break in the march, which did not occur, some sat down along the way to finish the food in their lunch baskets while others gave up and went to Washington Park, spread newspapers on the grass, and slept there until morning. Ultimately, most people got beyond the gates all right; but once on Cottage Grove Avenue, they were met by one filled cable car after another, because it had become popular to board cars in the opposite direction and keep the seats thus secured for the trip downtown. Two to three hundred people returned to the gates and asked the gatekeepers to allow them to sleep on the grass inside. They did. Long after midnight thousands were still massed at the end of Midway Plaisance waiting for cars; an equal number waited around Fifty-fifth Street. These were the conditions until 1 to 2 a.m.

For hours, a steady stream poured over the viaduct downtown. The Congress Street Alley "L" station was a solid mass of humanity until after midnight, and Michigan Avenue was blocked even later. With the Illinois Central, Elevated, steamboats, cable roads, and scores of other conveyances bringing people downtown from the fairgrounds, the crowds at midnight eclipsed anything previously seen on the streets of Chicago.

Cleaning Up After the Crowd

At midnight after the revelers had departed, Jackson Park was very much the worse for wear. Three-quarters of a million people had left behind a trail of debris. The lawns and plazas were covered with papers, bags, boxes, and the remnants of an infinite feast; the pathways were so littered that the *Daily News* said "it looked as though it must have snowed." The sanitation department began a desperate effort to clean up. Between midnight and dawn, no fewer than 500 well-packed wagonloads of trash were collected, loaded, and hauled to the southern end of the grounds. The job was overwhelming.

When the early visitors came pouring into the grounds on October 10, they were greeted by windrows of trash and hundreds of men with wagons, shovels, and sweepers, who were trying their best to make the park presentable for North Dakota Day, also Firemen's Day. Soon it appeared a miracle had occurred; and although there were still paper-pickers giving last touches to the transformation, the roads and lawns looked as clean and fresh as any previous morning.

The *Herald* reported that many unusual things were left behind by the crowd: "overcoats and table casters, fur shoulder capes and catalogues, umbrellas and souvenir badges, pocket flasks and guide books, tobacco pouches and canes, straw hats and satchels, pug dogs and babies." These and many other things were taken to the lost and found department. Listed in the *Tribune* were 15 pocketbooks with money, 25 umbrellas, 100 women's wraps, 5 overcoats, 10 pairs of spectacles, 5 satchels, 10 women's shopping bags, 5 railroad tickets, and enough odd gloves to sink an electric launch. The superintendent of lost and found believed these represented only about one-tenth of what was lost, as he had 2000 claims and only found one in ten of the lost articles.

Why Did So Many People Attend Chicago Day?

Regarding the stupendous attendance, the *Tribune* printed views of important World's Columbian Exposition officials:

> Director-General Davis felt, 'In the first place, this is a grand Exposition that is worth any one's time to see. Again, it was well advertised, and much credit is due the Council committee. Ald. Kerr's committee had a great deal more to do with bringing the people here than the Exposition. Then the railroads helped out by giving low fares. But, like everybody else, the crowd exceeded my expectations. I had thought that 500,000 people might come.'
>
> President Higinbotham thought it was 'easy to account for the large attendance. Chicago business houses were all closed. The railroads lowered their rates. There were excellent transportation facilities to and from the grounds. The show was well advertised and nothing was left undone to create public interest. Yes, there were more people than I expected. My guess had long been 500,000 plus.'
>
> Director Charles Henrotin agreed with Davis and added, 'It must not be forgotten, too, that there was much sentiment in creating the crowd. There were many thousands of people who knew of the fire and how Chicago had grown up for it. They knew that this day was commemorative of the great conflagration and they talked about it to their neighbors, and expected, of course, that something great would be done on such an important anniversary. Again, there were thousands of tickets purchased and not used because of just this sentiment.'
>
> Vice President Peck said, 'It was a great display of patriotism, and has done much for Chicago. I think there were 200,000 people went to Jackson Park yesterday who would not have gone but for their enthusiasm for the city. I could safely venture that many people put themselves at great discomfort in order to attest their good will.'

What Newspapers Around the Nation Said About Chicago Day

In column after column, Chicago newspapers of October 10 and 11 reprinted headlines and excerpts of articles from newspapers around the country that both congratulated Chicago on the resounding success of its day and gave an independent account of the event. Many had sent their own reporters to Jackson Park; and each described the astounding size of the crowd, the civic pride, and the marvelous sights. The Pittsburgh *Dispatch* comment is representative: "The entire country admires the spirit of enterprise which characterizes Chicago and will join in hearty congratulations at the manner in which she wiped out the last debt of the great show and cleared the decks for a large profit. The entire civilized world should be proud of Chicago." And from the *Kansas City Star*: "The one thought was 'we must beat Paris.' And they did it handsomely. That is the sort of enthusiasm and energy that makes a great America and a great West. Long live Chicago and long live a city's best friends—local pride and public spirit." The accolades went on and on.

For over a month prior, the newspapers gave Chicago Day a grand buildup. The day came and went in a blaze of glory. It is improbable that a U.S. newspaper of any size failed to report the result in its issue of October 10, 1893. The euphoria lasted three days, and then Chicago Day was forgotten by reporters, who turned to writing about daily events at the fair and plans for Manhattan Day, October 21.

Our story of Chicago Day is pieced together from sometimes conflicting newspaper accounts of the day. Many of the articles had to have been written in haste and from different perspectives in Jackson Park, so the interpretations and views of the day's activities were colored by what could be seen by the reporter. No one present at the fair could possibly have gotten the full picture. There also appears to have been selective reporting: the crowds depicted in photographs taken on Chicago Day often show sufficient space to move about, yet the reports suggest the park was totally clogged. Journalists of the day probably described the worst conditions they encountered to heighten the human drama.

It was, at the time, the greatest day in the history of Chicago and remained the greatest day of the World's Columbian Exposition.

Chicago Day Evening Scene on the Grand Plaza — Looking East Towards the Court of Honor (J. B. Campbell)

There is sufficient space to move about on the plaza, although a crowd is gathering at the Basin.

RECORD BREAKER!
713,646

The Chicago Daily Tribune.

RECORD BREAKER!
208,671

VOLUME LII.—NO. 283. TUESDAY, OCTOBER 10, 1893—SIXTEEN PAGES. PRICE TWO CENTS.

Tribune Front Page for October 10, 1893

GAS BALLOONING IN THE GAY '90s

By Ruth Owen Jones*

The *A. J. Myer* Balloon

Chicago Day dawned clear with only a little wind, and by afternoon there was a gentle breeze from the east, onshore from Lake Michigan. It was an ideal day for a balloon ascent, a calm day when the balloon would not be in danger of drifting out over the Lake.

Just before 4 p.m., Samuel Yates Baldwin attached himself to the trapeze below the recently built military balloon. The balloon had been filled part way using a hydrogen field generator and the rest of the way with hydrogen from the pressurized eight-foot long, five-inch diameter, seventy-pound gas cylinders, newly invented in England, which could be hauled on wagons. With his more experienced, famous, and heavier brother, Thomas Sackett Baldwin, in charge on the ground, the lighter weight Sam lifted off to the delight and rousing cheers of the crowd. From his starting point near the Government Building at the lakeshore, he drifted noiselessly southwest over the fair, over the Administration Building and Machinery Hall up, up, and up to 1500 feet. He had never gone up in front of such an enormous and noisy throng. They looked like moving ants to him, but he was not afraid, "No, not in the least," he said. He had never had a serious accident in his few short but active years of exhibition ballooning.

Preparing the "General Myer" on Chicago Day

Baldwin in the Trapeze of the "General Myer"

The 13,000-cubic-foot translucent balloon, full of volatile hydrogen, was made in Paris from dozens of bullock intestines which were beaten, stretched, and cured. These "gold-beaters' skins" were washed and impregnated with fish glue, then hand sewn together by women in six separate criss-crossed layers over an oiled cotton balloon. Between the middle layers was a lattice of crisscrossed bullock skin ribbons for reinforcement. When the skins dried, the heavy cotton inner balloon was removed. Baldwin had originally been asked to carry a flare-lit American Flag with him at dusk over the fair; but that foolish idea was scrapped, since the hydrogen

* Ruth Owen Jones, M.Ed., M.A. in American History, is a historical writer and picture researcher from Amherst, Massachusetts. She is also a thousand-hour instrument-rated private pilot who writes about the aviation history of New England.

and the balloon itself were highly flammable.

The U.S. Government Signal Corps balloon Baldwin was using had been named—and the name was emblazoned around the lower half—the *Signal Corps U.S. Army : Balloon : A. J. Myer.* It was the first balloon bought for the recently reestablished Signal Corps, the first government balloon and Signal Corps since the Civil War when tethered balloons were used by both the North and the South for spying, observing, and signaling directions from aloft using hand signals or telegraph. The new balloon was named for Albert J. Myer, the Civil War General who was Chief of the Union Signal Corps. The *General Myer,* as it was popularly known, was built in France using the latest English and French designs, which were thought technologically superior to those in this country. The new French-designed trapeze suspension mechanism seemed to minimize the basket's spinning motion. The fabric of the balloon was of English design.

Just as Sam Baldwin sailed quietly past the outside of the fairgrounds, he yanked on the rope that freed him and his parachute from the balloon above. The silk parachute and Baldwin came down quite slowly and landed safely on the roof of a shed near the railroad tracks at Sixty-seventh Street. Balloon chasers retrieved the *General Myer* six blocks south of the fair where it had descended. The Baldwins were famous for ballooning exhibitions and parachute jumping all over the American West, but also toured Japan, China, Southeast Asia, and India.

The experimental Chicago Day ascent was a good public relations and photo opportunity for the Signal Corps and the U.S. Government which had spent 8,000 francs or nearly $2,000 on the balloon. Congress appropriated the money, having been convinced that France and England were dangerously far ahead of the United States militarily with their balloons. The French army even had the new dirigibles—self-directed, motorized, more sausage-like balloons.

The Signal Corps had enlisted Tom and Sam Baldwin of Quincy, Illinois, to manage the new balloon at the fair. The *General Myer* arrived from France that May, but there was a delay in the arrival of the gas cylinders which were not delivered until early October. The fair was nearly over, and few people knew how to demonstrate the balloon. In 1891 the Baldwins had decreased their tours of the world with their balloons and had bought part of the Quincy fairgrounds, renaming it Baldwin Park. There was a race course, grandstand, bowling alley, and baseball diamond; and there were frequent Baldwin balloon and parachute exhibitions.

At the end of Chicago Day, a swaggering Sam Baldwin told a *Chicago Daily Tribune* reporter, "Well, I guess I've seen more of the crowd at the Fair today than anyone else. I would not have missed today's experience for a great deal. Perhaps I shall not have another chance to ascend before such a large crowd as long as I live."

The *General Myer* was a popular success. On October 25, with Tom Baldwin in control on the ground and Sergeant Creighton in the basket, the Corps demonstrated the use of the new telephone with the balloon via an insulated electrical tether line. More demonstrations followed at the fair, twenty of them on the final day, October 30. The *General Myer* was then sent to Fort Riley, Kansas, for use in Signal Corps training.

The Balloon *Eagle Eyrie*

The *Eagle Eyrie* was another balloon seen at the fair (see candid photo #20). It was the often free-ranging balloon of Samuel Archer King of Philadelphia, the foremost balloonist in the country from 1860 to 1900. King had been invited to the fair to help with the Signal Corps' *General Myer* demonstrations but may not have been there when that balloon was finally ready in October.

Samuel King began making exhibition flights in Philadelphia in 1851 and was a regular for Fourth of July entertainment in the northeast. In 1858 he introduced the drag rope to ballooning to regulate the ascent and for helpers to use in assisting. In 1860 he introduced aerial photography with a series of pictures over Boston Common taken by James Wallace Black from King's tethered balloon, the *Queen of the Air*. "Boston as the Eagle and Wild Goose See It" is the title of the best photograph from that flight. King had made hundreds of ascents including a 400-mile flight in 1874 from Buffalo, New York, to Salem, New Jersey. He then proposed that crossing the Atlantic Ocean was possible. He was dubbed Professor King and was actually quite interested in scientific observations, not just commercial entertainment.

On September 22, 1893, State Commissioners' Day, King and his *Eagle Eyrie* were hired as a promotion to attract crowds. The balloon was on display at the fair between the New York State Building and the front of the Fine Arts Building. King had built the balloon himself in Philadelphia. It was a fine, blue-sky day at the fair with light east winds off the Lake. King planned to float west of the city where he could land on open prairie. He inflated his balloon at 3 p.m., using a field generator.

In the crowd was a young woman who was employed selling guides at Fine Arts, Miss Joie Morris from Ames, Iowa. She begged to accompany King in the basket of the balloon, and was at first rejected. Miss Morris had a "... pretty and persuasive manner," and King relented. At 3:45 p.m. the two ascended amid cheers of "Bon Voyage." They were, at first, blown slowly and quietly southwest on a gentle breeze. Professor King and Miss Morris waved happily to their friends and the crowd as they climbed higher and higher and outside the fairgrounds.

Unfortunately, at about 5000 feet, they hit an opposite wind direction, a stronger northeast wind current which carried them swiftly and frighteningly out over expansive Lake Michigan. The rescue cutter, *Andy Johnson*, put out after them, chased them a good distance as they were dragged over the surface of the water, and finally rescued them.

Where Joie Morris went is unknown; but Samuel King returned to Pennsylvania and continued to work with ballooning, weather observations, and Signal Corps training into the next century. Near the end of his years, he was even a passenger in an aeroplane.

The Captive Balloon on the Midway

The ballooning exhibits were located in the Transportation Building in Group 84, Class 526. The fair was produced to show off the superiority of the America Christopher Columbus had landed on in 1492, but at the time of the fair, the U.S. was not notable in ballooning and had not entered exhibits. France was the premier ballooning country in 1893, and although none of France's entries in any department at the fair were listed in the *Directory*, it had a balloon display. Cosmos Verlags und Verkehrsanstalt Company of Hanover, Germany, exhibited samples of their captive balloon. The emphasis in the Transportation Department was elsewhere: The chief, lawyer Willard Smith, was a railroad fan. Fully two-thirds of the floor space in his building was devoted to displays on railroading, an American success story. Steamships were the next biggest exhibit. The small showing of aeronautics included a life-sized statue of Joseph Michel Montgolfier who, with his brother, Jacques, invented the first practical balloon. Made of linen and inflated with hot air, it rose without passengers for ten minutes on July 5, 1783, in France.

Montgolfier Statue in the Transportation Building

The fair planners had said, "... it was determined to exclude a branch of invention (aeronautics) in which centuries of labor had accomplished so little practical result." Indeed, the practical uses for balloons were few in 1893. They had been used in wars since the 1790s in France; and they were being used for aerial photography, but the primary use for balloons was for entertainment. The dirigible or directable balloon was just being developed in Europe, and it would be in the next century that balloons would become more valuable for weather observations even up into the stratosphere.

As we have seen, ballooning was at the fair where good hydrogen could be obtained; and its most visible location was on the Midway as a curiosity. On the Midway Plaisance, built "... for the legitimate overflow of the exposition," past the newly invented Ferris Wheel, near the live ostrich farming exhibit, and across from the West African Dahomey Village, which was reputedly the loudest of the ethnic exhibits, was a tethered captive hydrogen balloon. From that height, a panoramic view of the fair, Lake Michigan, and the surrounding countryside could be had. On a very clear day, a 25-mile view was likely.

Despite the paucity of aeronautics displays in the Transportation Building, one extremely important step in the science of aerial navigation was taken at the Exposition. More than ten years before the Wright brothers flew at Kitty Hawk, one of the 210 congresses held at the fair was the Conference on Aerial Navigation, held August 1–4 in the Art Institute Building downtown. Scientists came from all over the world to present 45 different papers on balloon meteorology, design of a navigable balloon, manufacturing hydrogen balloons, and on the heavier-than-air machines of the future.

Looking East at the Captive Balloon Concession on the Midway
[Cold American Lunches and Dinners Were Available Aloft]

More important than the actual conference was the fact that the papers presented in those four days were published in a new journal called *Aeronautics*, which ran for 12 months over the period from October 1893 to September 1894. The Conference on Aerial Navigation at the Chicago world's fair was truly an important event.

PHOTOGRAPHY AND FAIRS

By Thomas Yanul*

All of the major expositions and fairs in the past, including the Columbian Exposition, had professional photographers to record both the ongoing construction and the finished product.

What we now call amateur photographers (those with little or no training) were in existence in significant numbers only a few years prior to the Exposition, so our subject matter here as historical reference is confined to the professional.

Briefly, certain standards of artistic commercial architectural photography were created with the introduction of iron construction made possible by the industrial revolution around the middle of the nineteenth century.

The first photographs to consider when discussing expositions are those of the 1851 Crystal Palace building, in London, England. Although that building was photographed at the time, it was not until the building's removal to Sydenham, England, reconstruction, and enlargement over the next four years that modern artistic exposition photography can be said to have existed. It was photographer Philip Henry Delamotte's 160 selected views of this Palace from 1852-54 that set a new standard for artistic commercial photography. His work created a visual aesthetic language that was far superior to a mere utilitarian record. It became a reference point for future photographers when recording large, monumental architectural structures.

The Crystal Palace, London. The First World's Fair, 1851.

The next landmark work occurred at the Universal Exposition in Paris, 1889. Although Gustave Eiffel's famous tower was more the public's "landmark" structure, it was really the great iron sheds built to house the exhibits that created the most artistic designs from the standpoint of creative record photography. The grand scale prints of the fair buildings made from 20- x 24-inch glass plates were a high point in exposition photography. They recorded, with great artistic sympathy, the eloquent designs that had been produced by engineers and architects at that fair. The photographer responsible for these distinctive images was Albert Chevojon, chief photographer for the commercial photography firm of Delmaet-Durandelle, established in Paris in 1861. Chevojon joined the firm in 1885, almost

* Thomas Yanul, 56, was born and raised in Chicago. He has been the chief photographic surveyor for the Illinois Historic Sites Survey, "banquet" photographer of large groups, free-lance photographer specializing in architectural preservation, and designer and builder of large format panoramic cameras. His latest show was in Paris, September and November 1996, at the Gallery of the Bibliotheque Historic de la Ville du Paris. He has studied the Chicago photographer George R. Lawrence, active in the 1890s; and his most recent research projects have dealt with C. D. Arnold, the official view photographer, and John J. Gibson, official portrait photographer, of the World's Columbian Exposition.

immediately becoming chief photographer. Chevojon became the eventual owner of the firm, and two additional generations of Chevojons have continued the work to this day.

Columbian Exposition Photography

Photography had for a long time been a commonly used tool for construction recording. Its utility, if not its artistic value, was prized for its relative low-cost, speed, and easy image duplication along with its unquestioned veracity.

Officials connected with the planning and execution of the World's Columbian Exposition were well aware of the utility of photographic recording, both as a tool for the dissemination of information and as a matter of historical record.

The initial site-planning work was recorded photographically by New York architectural photographer Charles Dudley Arnold beginning in the fall of 1890. By the time of the actual start of construction in February 1891, Arnold had been engaged as chief construction photographer for Director of Works, Daniel Burnham's department.

Other photographers did early work for the Exposition, including the well-known Chicago photographer J. W. Taylor. Some might argue that Taylor, or any number of other professional photographers in the area, should have gotten the work. The fact is no one knows why Arnold got the job and some other person did not; maybe they did not want the job, maybe they did not know the right people. The fact remains that Arnold pursued the contract and got it, a simple everyday commercial photography business arrangement. He was skilled in his craft, probably had good references, and knew some important architects. Some historians have hinted that this somehow is an immoral manner in which to find work.

C. D. Arnold, Canadian by birth, was 48 when he began work at the fair in 1890. His photographic background is too extensive to dwell on here; suffice it to say that it was suitable for the work at the Exposition.

Although dogged by a certain amount of criticism throughout the life of the fair, Arnold has been unjustly criticized for the most part by historians counting angels on the head of a pin. Most of the complications pertaining to the Department of Photography can be laid at the doorstep of too much work, too little time, and nettlesome bureaucracy from the likes of Director-General George R. Davis and professional gadfly F. C. Beach. Davis and the National Commission were a constant thorn in the Chicago Corporation's side, as they tried to have input in the running and direction of the Exposition; they were largely ignored by the Corporation, but Davis cried loud and long enough to finally make the Ways and Means Committee have Arnold bend to avoid continued uncomfortable press reports over this tempest-in-a-teapot affair.

Official Logo for the Department of Photography

The other chief Arnold antagonist throughout the fair was Frederick Converse Beach, a co-founder of the New York Amateur Photographers Club and founder of the *American Amateur Photographer Journal.* Beach considered himself the Joan of Arc of amateur photography and made it a cause célèbre to, first, try to get permission for amateur photographers to be represented as exhibitors; then, lobby for free use of any size camera by amateurs; and, finally, blame Arnold for everything and anything he considered wrong with photography at the fair. Arnold himself had wondered aloud to a press personage that he could not understand the hateful nature of Beach's constant diatribe against him, especially since the two had never met. Beach, a prominent businessman with a scientific education, was used to getting his way—absolutely. This trait, at least for me, answers the question of why his crusade of vengeance against Arnold had been so widespread and vituperative.

Needless to say, in hindsight, Arnold did create a most memorable set of grand views of the Exposition's buildings and grounds, as had been his main responsibility. In spite of mishandling by later bureaucrats and subsequent loss of the original negatives, a sufficient enough record was preserved of this superb architectural undertaking whose life was so fleeting but never forgotten by those who saw it.

C. D. Arnold's professional work at the Columbian Exposition was a continuation of the grand and eloquent style of previous exposition photographers. His contribution, along with that of the previously mentioned photographers, has left us with a legacy of the artistic visual language of the now vanished monumental Exposition architecture.

A Second Official Logo for the Department of Photography

At the time of the Columbian Exposition, genuine amateur photography was just beginning to become a reality. One cannot help but believe that work such as Arnold's and that of other fair photographers, though formal and technically advanced, had some effect on amateur "snapshooters" who maybe hoped that one day they could produce such elegant images. In the meantime, their own candid and informal camera work would change the way Americans viewed their world.

The grandeur of the Exposition and the delightfulness of the Midway curiosities intrigued a new generation of photographers whose exploits excited their friends and family. The tradition of taking snapshots to form a personal pictorial diary has been going on for more than a century. Today, automation makes photography easier and less expensive, and the emotional investment in the photographic process has changed. The excitement of making one's own photographs is unknown to many, and photography, for some, is an everyday hobby requiring little thought or understanding. Familiarity has bred its share of contempt.

The genuine wonder evoked at nineteenth century expositions will never be replicated, nor will the feeling of being an amateur photographer today ever match the giddy thrills of those experimenters and hobbyists in the early years.

"We can never go home again," so the saying goes.

ଓଓ — ଊଊ

ABOUT THE CANDID PHOTOGRAPHS

Presented here are the facts and circumstances known about the candid world's fair photographs reproduced in the next chapter.

There are 58 photographs in the cache, which was purchased from a bookstore in Boston, Massachusetts. Each print is uniformly glued on an eighth-inch-thick embossed professional card mount which measures 7¾ x 10 inches. The buff fronts have a recessed area in the center measuring 5 x 6½ inches; inside this is a printed tan frame, which serves as a border to each mounted 4- x 5-inch photograph. Every photo is landscape oriented except one; and all are neatly and expertly mounted, except two that were torn slightly during mounting. The cards are similar to popular Victorian cabinet photographs.

An Example of One of the Mounted Candid Platinum Photographs

There are 43 different photographs in the set, all of which are presented here. The photographer printed multiple copies of print #3 (2 copies), #6 (2), #7 (2), #10 (2), #8 (3), #35 (2), #36 (2), #37 (2), #38 (5), #41 (2), and #42 (2). Since the copies have different degrees of brightness and contrast, evidently the photographer was experimenting with the print parameters of exposure and development. It is important to the story that the photographer had access to the negatives. Overall, the prints have high contrast and tend to be dark, but show fine detail. No pictures are blurred or out of focus; since tripods were not allowed on the grounds, this shows that the photographer was experienced enough to carefully prop or steady his camera. The photographs must have been stored in uneven stacks untouched for a long period of time, since the exposed surfaces of the mounts and images were dirty. Requiring only a gentle cleaning with a gum eraser, the 100-year-old photographs are in excellent condition and give us some unique views of the Exposition.

The back of each mount is gray and unmarked by any company logo. A number of the backs are inscribed with a soft-lead pencil in one person's handwriting. They include:

#3-	"Administration Bldg" "Chicago Day" "716000 Paid Admissions"
#6-	"Manufactures & Liberal Arts Bldg"
#7-	"The Manufactures & Liberal Arts Building"
#13, and #14-	"U S Government Bldg"
#25-	"Illinois State Bldg"
#30-	"Horticultural Bldg"
#43-	"Agricultural Bldg"

We know our photographer only by the initials "H. R. P. 2d," which is neatly printed in pencil on the lower right corner of the tan border in photographs #28 and #38.

We know some properties of the camera HRP used at the fair. The field of view and vantage point in the photographs were plotted on a copy of the accurate Heinze architectural map of the Exposition grounds, which is reproduced and placed at the end of this book. From this we learned that each photo has the same angular field of about 38 degrees, hence, only one lens was used.

The photo illustrations in the souvenir book, *Glimpses of the World's Fair,* were "taken with a No. 4 Kodak," as stated on the verso of the title page. There are several illustrations in *Glimpses* taken from nearly the same vantage point chosen by HRP, so that a comparison of view angles can be made. The illustrations show that HRP's camera had a lens nearly identical to the Kodak No. 4 (illustrated in *Image*; see Reference List).

Camera Permit for the Duke of Veragua and His Son, Descendants of Columbus

George Eastman had invented roll film in 1888 and provided development and printing for it; these quickly made photography easy for the novice, since fragile glass plates and home processing were no longer needed. He exhibited his Kodak cameras, film, and prints at the 1889 Paris Exposition, winning a gold medal. His goal was putting photography in the consumer's hands. At the Columbian Exposition, Kodak exhibited photographs and equipment and also had a "Free Dark Room" where cameras could be rented.

The No. 4 was manufactured from 1890 to 1897. It had a one-inch diameter Bausch & Lomb lens with average focal length of about nine inches, adjustable shutter, and rotating f-stops. It came in box or folding form and was pre-loaded with 48 to 200 exposures of 4- x 5-inch roll film or equipped with plate back. For visitors, 4- x 5-inch format cameras were the largest allowed on the fairgrounds. The No. 4 folding Kodak—sometimes referred to as the "Columbus" model—had the same lens and approximate focal length as the box version. It, too, could be adapted for roll or plate film. Kodak would develop, print, and mount the images for the photographer; but negatives were not returned. HRP must have developed his own, since duplicates were made from some of the images, and "Kodak" is not printed on the mounts.

Using the above dimensions for the No. 4 and trigonometry, we can find the approximate field of view:

$$\text{Angle of view (degrees)} = 2 \times [90° - \tan^{-1} (2 \times \text{focal length} \div (\text{film width} + \text{lens width}))]$$

From this formula, the angle of view of the No. 4 is about 37 degrees, which agrees remarkably well with the angle found for the candid photographs—about 38 degrees—and the No. 4 photographs published in *Glimpses*. Kodak made other cameras in 1893; could they have been used? Kodak advertised their No. 1 as having a field of view of 60 degrees and the No. 3 as having 42 degrees. The No. 1 made round pictures and the No. 3 made prints 3¼ x 4¼ inches, so neither of these models took the candid photographs. The actual camera used by HRP is unknown, but it had the properties of the Kodak No. 4.

Developing and Printing Photographs in 1893

What developing and printing technology was available to the experienced amateur photographer, someone like HRP, in 1893? W. F. Carlton's book, *The Amateur Photographer : A Complete Guide For Beginners*, 1894 edition, gives some of the possibilities.

Although it is possible that HRP used a spool of film, it is more likely that he used glass plates mounted in holders, two plates to a holder. HRP's 58 prints are crisp right to the edge of the image; with roll film one might expect occasional fuzziness at the edges due to curling of the film. After exposure, the plates would have been wrapped in orange paper and stored until he returned to his darkroom to develop them.

Developing Plates

HRP's darkroom was quite orderly. Once in this room, and before closing the door, he organized his work area and prepared his "developer" and "fixing" solutions. He lit his ruby lantern filled with "astral (or any good kerosene)" and shut out all other light. Only then did he unwrap the sets of 4- x 5-inch plates he had so carefully wrapped before leaving Chicago and proceed to develop them by placing them in a tray and covering them with diluted commercial developer.

Carlton's *Amateur Photographer*

Applying about three ounces of developer per 4- x 5-inch plate, he took care to cover them with one sweep, rocking the tray to keep them evenly covered. As he watched closely, faint outlines of familiar Exposition buildings appeared. Within minutes, the skies darkened; and as he held them up to his ruby lamp, he became justifiably proud of the quality of the developing plates. No matter how many photographs he took, this revelation that he had actually captured a scene never failed to excite him. As the objects came clearly into his view, he was filled with the memories of his fine trip to Chicago.

The plates were now negatives, ready for washing in cold water before fixing. Ahead of time, he had prepared his fixative, "Hypo" for hyposulfite of soda. He placed his negatives in a second tray, covered them with this solution, and rocked them back and forth for one minute after the yellow opaqueness as seen from the back had completely disappeared. He then washed the negatives thoroughly with cold water and placed them in a negative rack to air dry.

Printing on Platinum Paper

Three photographic archivists concur that HRP's prints are on platinum paper. This adds credence to the conclusion that HRP was a knowledgeable amateur or perhaps even an unknown professional. Platinum papers were available after about 1885 and were prized for their tonal values and stable images. The price to be paid for these advantages was the need for specialized chemicals and the higher cost of the print paper. A printing frame and contact process were used. These operations could be performed in moderate light, since the paper was not extremely sensitive. Enlargers, as we know them, were unknown in 1893.

Carlton's *Amateur Photographer* booklet did not have a printing and developing process for platinum prints—also called platinotype, but the procedure can be found in *Wall's Dictionary of Photography.* The contact printing chemistry is based on the reduction of ferric salt to a ferrous salt by the action of light; the ferrous salt is, in turn, made to reduce a platinum compound to metallic platinum. Platinum forms the final image and is far more permanent than any print having a silver image. Toning, necessary for many silver-based images, is not required. No emulsion is used, so the picture lies on the natural surface of the paper, allowing prints of distinctive character.

HRP may have purchased pre-coated paper or made his own. If he made his own, he may have used high quality paper or drawing paper sized with gelatin, alum, and methylated spirit. If he sized the paper, he then thoroughly dried it before coating with the sensitizing solutions. The three sensitizing solutions are oxalic acid plus ferric oxalate, oxalic acid plus ferric oxalate and potassium chlorate, and a solution of potassium chlorplatinite. Depending on the contrast desired, HRP mixed certain amounts of each solution and poured the resulting mixture from an egg-cup into a pool in the center of each paper. He then brushed the solution until it evenly covered the paper and the paper was dry. In almost total darkness, he next dried the paper until it crackled when flexed. He would have carried out the coating process in ordinary room light; but unless he was going to use the sensitized paper immediately, he stored it in a dark place (a calcium tube).

To print, he worked from the back of the frame, positioning his negative film side up, covering it with dry sensitized paper and a sheet of India rubber. He then carefully latched the frame, taking care not to break the negative. He took the frames with his thick negatives into direct sunlight for developing and placed his thin negatives in subdued light. He checked the print process by loosening one corner of the printing frame, bending back the paper from the negative to view the sensitized paper. If the negative was of normal density, printing took about five minutes in the sun. When the image was visible in a brownish-gray color and the unexposed margins had remained yellow, he knew the paper had been sufficiently exposed. He replaced the back-boards on those not sufficiently printed and continued the exposure until he was satisfied. When a print was complete, he placed it in a dark box.

The prints were developed at room temperature by immersing them for one or two minutes in a potassium oxalate solution, the action of which caused the reduction of the platinum compound wherever a ferrous salt existed. The developer could be mixed with small amounts of other chemicals (potassium phosphate or mercuric chloride) to modify the degree of reduction of the platinum, hence changing the gray scale (warmth) of the print. Unwanted residual chemicals were then thoroughly cleared in a 1½ percent hydrochloric acid solution, and the print water-washed then dried or mounted.

HRP mounted the wet prints by laying them face down on glass, coating the back of the top one with paste, and placing the print in the center of a card-mount obtained from a photographic supplier. He smoothed the print out from the center to the edges by laying a sheet of paper over it and rubbing with the palm of the hand, taking care not to tear it. HRP tore a corner of two prints ever so slightly during this process.

Questions About the Photographs

Although the 43 photographs plus duplicates represent a large group with a theme, "Chicago Day," we do not know if they are a complete set. For instance, there are only two photographs taken on the Midway, and they are not of the most impressive exhibits. Why were photographs not taken of Streets of Cairo, German Village, or the giant Ferris Wheel? Also, why were no state buildings and only two foreign buildings included? Why were no photographs taken of the Chicago Day parade and the extensive evening festivities. These missing "standard" photographs might be explained by HRP's not having enough time, not having enough film, the crowd obscuring the big events, or lack of light; any of which could have happened. Also, HRP may have only printed and mounted his selected best photographs. Or some cards may have been lost or destroyed.

If HRP used a Kodak No. 4, he had some means since it cost about $55 with film, the Exposition required a $2-a-day or $5-a-week permit to take pictures on the grounds, and he needed a dark room and chemicals. C. D. Arnold and Harlow D. Higinbotham, son of the president of the Exposition, held the official photography concession at no fee. As a monetary reference point, in the depression of 1893–94, the 50-cent admission price for the World's Columbian Exposition was considered by many to be expensive.

C. D. ARNOLD

AND

HARLOW D. HIGINBOTHAM.

CHICAGO, ILL.

AGREEMENT.

21st APRIL, 1893.

RIGHT TO ESTABLISH A BUREAU OF PHOTOGRAPHY AND MAKE AND SELL PHOTOGRAPHS OF THE GROUNDS AND BUILDINGS OF THE WORLD'S COLUMBIAN EXPOSITION.

CHICAGO:
PRINTED BY THE CHICAGO LEGAL NEWS COMPANY.
1893.

Columbian Photography Concession Contract

The photographs generate another question: were they all taken on Chicago Day or did they span several days? Most of the photos show huge crowds which would be expected on the largest attendance day of the fair. However, photographs #10, #23, #30, and #37 do not show such crowds. Some seem to have been taken on a cloudy day, and the direction of the flags flying from the buildings do not always point in the same direction as in other photos; but this could be from changing weather conditions, which appears to be the case from comparisons with published pictures taken on Chicago Day. No print shows clouds because of the film sensitivity to blue and ultraviolet. Thus, shadow length and direction and the published program were used to determine the sequence of the pictures.

We have organized and numbered the photographs as though they were all taken on October 9, 1893, with HRP following the schedule of events for that day and participating just as most visitors did at that festive event. We have imagined the dialogue and commentary among HRP and two women with him (see candid photograph #18) as they explored the fairgrounds. The sequence of the photographs is our best estimate for "a walk with our photographer" around the grounds as accomplished in a day. The tour is fictional but the facts and comments are accurate to the best of our knowledge.

A reproduction of an accurate Heinze folding map accompanying this book shows HRP's vantage points and view angles in red; the numbers correspond to those assigned to the photographs. To aid the reader's orientation during the tour, each photograph is provided with a Heinze map vignette reduced to 55 percent showing HRP's location and angle of view for that photograph. Each photograph has been enlarged to 130 percent of its original size except #21 and #22 (110 percent).

As an additional aid, a simpler map showing the route the group took about the fairgrounds is illustrated on the next page.

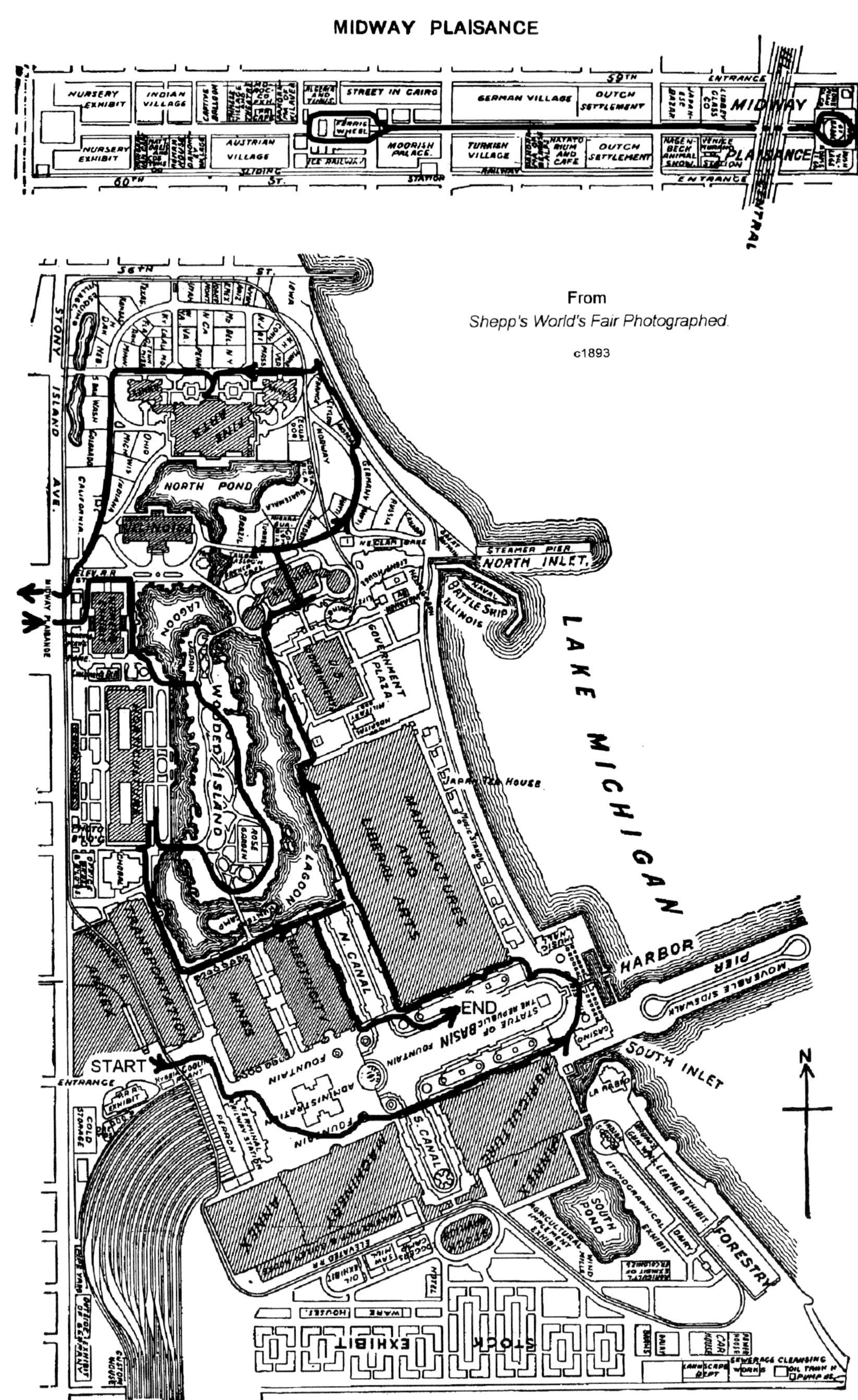
MIDWAY PLAISANCE
From
Shepp's World's Fair Photographed.
c1893
START
END
LAKE MICHIGAN
NORTH POND
WOODED ISLAND
LAGOON
GOVERNMENT PLAZA
MANUFACTURES AND LIBERAL ARTS
STEAMER PIER
NORTH INLET
SOUTH INLET
HARBOR
BASIN
STOCK EXHIBIT
FORESTRY
SOUTH POND
N

A WALK WITH OUR PHOTOGRAPHER

"My, what a glorious day, but it surely took a long time to get in here," remarked Harald R. Philip, turning to his wife and mother after buying admission tickets. He had bought a *Rand, McNally & Co.'s Hand Book* guide to the fair from the World's Fair Novelty Stand the previous day. Knowing their time would be brief on Chicago Day because of Mother's age, he had taken Sunday to get a $5 camera permit, become acquainted with the fairgrounds, and pick out his photographic vantage points. He was excited about snapping views of the marvelous buildings and being a part of the holiday celebration.

"Millicent, I want to capture the main entrance as people pour in," he said to his wife. As he stepped up on a ledge, he thought, "This area to the side of Terminal Station is great. Colorful flags are flying in the breeze, and people are dressed up and so jolly. The Transportation, Horticulture in the distance, and Mines Buildings are all in my view." He turned to Violet and asked, "Mother, do you want a rolling chair?" The concession was to their far left.

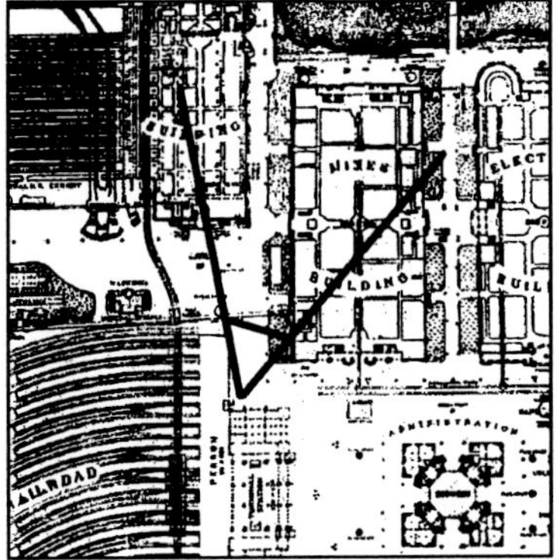

"No, Son, it's a nice day for a walk," she answered.

"Look at all the folks trying to get into Hayward's Restaurant. I'm glad we brought a picnic lunch. To save time we may want to buy fruit at the stands like the one I see over there," he suggested as he pointed to the kiosk near the corner of the Transportation Building.

#1

Transportation **Fruit Stand** **Horticulture** **Hayward's Restaurant in Front of Mines** **Ore Rail Scaffolding**

#2

Mines Building Soda Water Stand Electricity Building Manufactures Chocolat-Menier

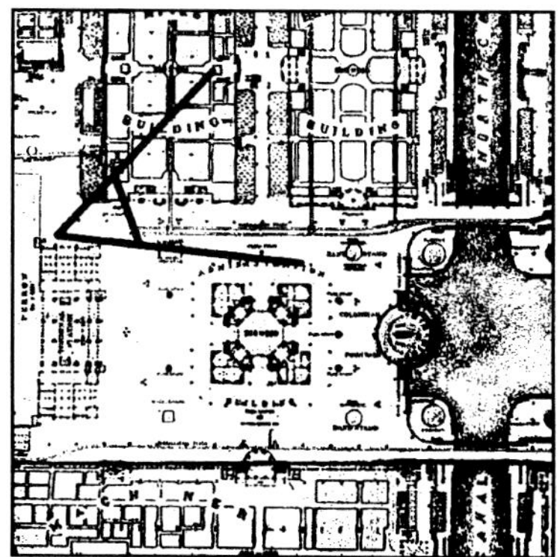

"From this handy spot by the Station, I'll swing around to the east. The throng makes a nice addition to the fronts of the Mines and Electricity Buildings. In the distance, I can see the long elegant sweep of the Manufactures Building extending all the way down to the Peristyle. On the very right, I can get a good view of the Chocolat-Menier building and exhibit—my, it smells great even from here!" Harald exclaimed as he steadied for the shot.

Millicent read from the guidebook, "The Mines Building is 350 by 700 feet long and the Electricity Building nearly the same. What a handsome pair, especially with the tall electric lamps out front stretched out in a row all the way down to Music Hall by the Peristyle."

"I'm pleased there are soda water stands like that one at the corner of the Mines Building," said Mother. "I can see that folks are thirsty already."

"Who designed the Mines Building, Millicent?" asked Harald.

"S. S. Beman from Chicago. The inspiration was Italian Renaissance, but the exterior design has a French spirit to it. The second floor galleries are 60 feet wide. Frederick J. V. Skiff is the department chief," she answered, reading on.

"Well," remarked Harald, as he hopped down, "let's go over to the Administration Building to see the New Liberty Bell."

FROM THE
World's Fair NoVelty Stand,
57 ST. & STONEY ISLAND AV.,
THE LARGEST STOCK OF
WORLD'S FAIR GOODS
In the City.

Purple Stamp on the Title Page of Millicent's *Hand Book* Guide

#3

New Liberty Bell in Front of the West Entrance of the Administration Building

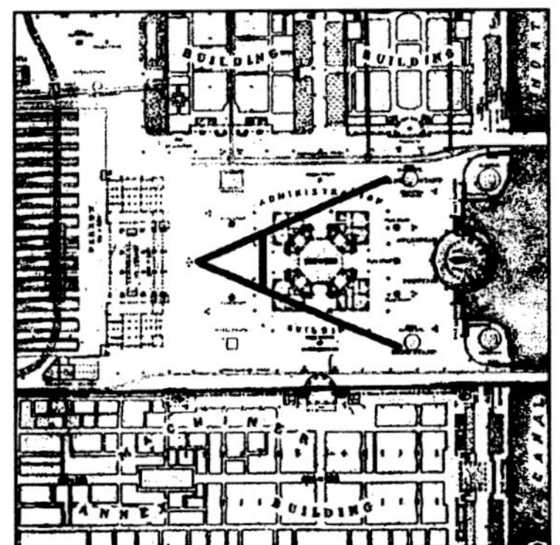

"Look at this sea of people! I think the noon festivities are just over, but I can't see for sure," said Millicent as they arrived in front of the west entrance to the Administration Building.

"This is certainly a grand place and symbol for the offices which control the Exposition," said Mother, admiring the expansive entrance.

"The second floor balcony gives a great view, and the dome is bronzed aluminum, so it can be seen for miles," reported Millicent from the guidebook. She continued, "It was designed by Richard Morris Hunt, and the sculptures I see on it are by Karl Bitter. Inside are the offices for the administration officials, and fire and police departments. The Northern Trust Company Bank of Chicago conducts a model bank inside, plus there is a restaurant too."

"Can you get a view of the top of Administration?" asked Millicent. "It's 275 feet high."

"I'm too close now. Maybe some other time," answered her husband, watching the restless crowd. "What a great design for a building. It looks commanding, inviting, and open. I can see past the west entrance arches right through to the east arches and beyond. Spacious." He peered over the crowd and exclaimed, "There it is!—The New Liberty Bell on its sturdy oak frame right in front of Administration. See how they've unfurled a flag from one corner, and look at the people still up on the frame and on the light bases where they viewed the ceremonies. For my picture, I'll get up on this light base to get above the crowd." When finished, he jumped down and led them away. "I'd like to get a better view of the Bell."

#4

New Liberty Bell Bitter Sculpture West Entrance of Administration

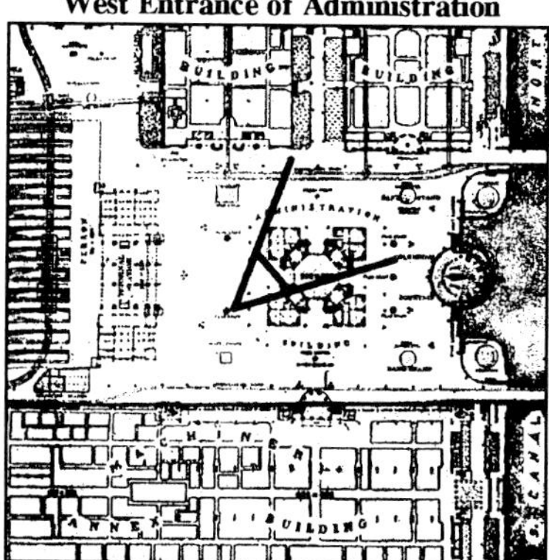

"I need to get closer," said Harald. "Come over to the next light base with me."

"Be careful Son, there are many visitors rushing by," said the older woman.

"Oh, Mother, look, there is a family in front of me with a lunch basket, and before the Bell in his chair is one of the uniformed guides for the Columbia Rolling Chair Company. Folks don't seem to know which activity or part of the park they want to go to next," said Harald, taking steady aim from his perch. "From here I see the same men are doggedly hanging onto their positions on the bell frame and lamp bases."

"The Bell surely has been popular this summer, judging from the newspaper reports," piped in Millicent. "It has been rung on many occasions to symbolize unity and celebration. Today it'll get a good workout!"

"What is the sculpture just to the left of the Administration entrance?" asked Harald.

"Let's see," murmured Millicent, paging through the book. "It's 'Earth' by Bitter; the other three elements on the other three sides are 'Fire, Water, and Air.' I hope the inscription above the entrance is legible in your photograph."

"I'll try to keep it in the view," replied Harald, taking the picture carefully.

"Now it's time to go around to the other side of the Administration Building where other activities are being held," said Harald, jumping down from his perch and motioning to the two women to follow.

#5

East Facade of Administration **Bandstand in Front of the South Entrance of the Electricity Building** **Women With Lunch Basket**

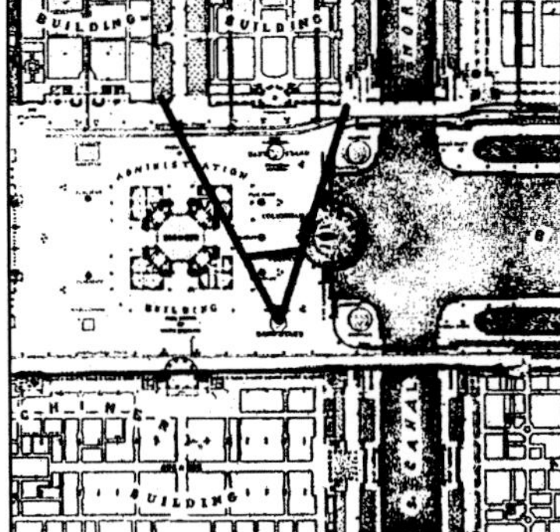

"Look at this grand panorama," exalted Millicent as they rounded the south corner of the Administration Building.

"Yes," agreed Harald. "I think I can best capture it by getting up to the top floor of the bandstand here and taking pictures across the Plaza. Wait for me."

When he came down a short while later, he reported on the series of pictures he had just taken. "The first looks straight at the opposite bandstand where I could see lots of other spectators getting a better look too. They were directly in front of the Electricity Building, so I couldn't see the statue by Carl Rohl-Smith of Ben Franklin harnessing lightning. But the facade is very imposing and inviting. Lots of visitors are sitting and waiting for the activities. It's good they brought their umbrellas—the sun is mighty warm for October. I also saw a happy quartet of ladies arm-in-arm and carrying a lunch basket. The three massive flag poles with ornate bases make an imposing show at the east entrance of Administration, don't they?"

"I like the statue of Columbus which is there also," added Millicent.

Harald agreed, and said sorrowfully, "It wasn't in any of my views."

Franklin Statue at the Electricity Building Entrance

#6

South Entrance of the Electricity Electric Fountain MacMonnies Fountain Manufactures in Background

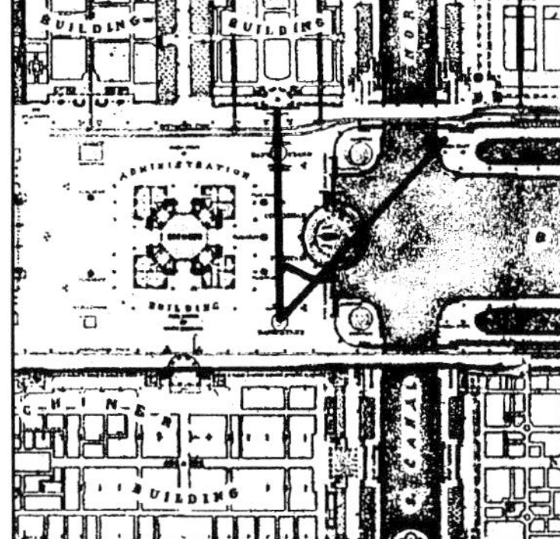

He continued, “Next, I turned a bit to the right to see not only the Electricity Building, but also MacMonnies’ grand allegorical fountain and the huge Manufactures and Liberal Arts Building looming behind the fountain. I could also see the Edison Company’s electric fountains shooting colored streams of sparkling water gaily into the air and— ”

Mother interrupted, “Do you like MacMonnies’ design?”

Millicent answered by saying, “It’s an imposing piece commemorating Columbus’ voyage of exploration. And it certainly is placed in an advantageous location, yet it seems too fanciful and ornate. They say it’s similar to the one designed and implemented for the 1889 Paris fair. I’m sure the long voyage in uncharted waters would better be remembered and portrayed as exciting, dangerous, tense, and exhausting.”

MacMonnies Fountain

“Well, I guess Columbus would stand amazed on his fountain if he could view the Manufactures Building before him and the Machinery Building, which powers this fair, behind him. As the largest building, Manufactures is 787 feet wide and 1687 long, making it nearly 31 acres according to the guidebook,” interjected Harald. “I’ve forgotten, who designed such a colossal thing?”

“George Post of New York, it says here,” came the answer. “See how the cornice is the same height as the surrounding buildings, making this all seem like a city with a purpose.”

Electricity Building **Electric Fountain** **MacMonnies Fountain** **Crowd Atop Manufactures**

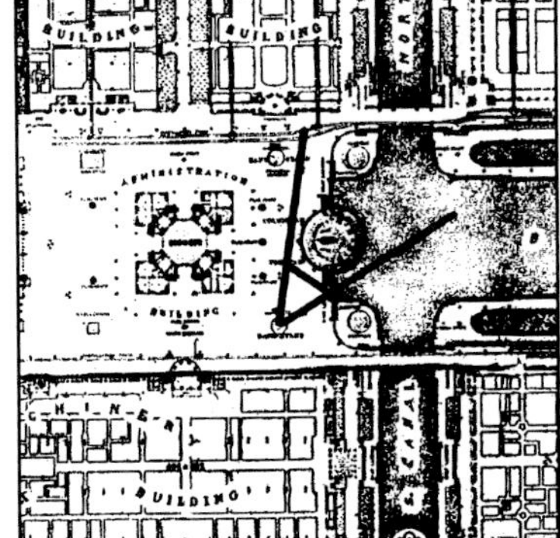

"I was headed down from the bandstand when I noticed that big crowd gathered on the south roof of Manufactures," Harald pointed up. "Now that's a vantage point! With all these people it's difficult to see today's events, but up there it's possible to see the entire grounds. The bandstand railing was a good place to rest my camera, so I took another picture to show more of the people on the promenade. I wish we had time to go up there and examine the giant searchlights on the west corners of the roof," continued Harald.

"How do they get up there?" asked Mother.

"The guidebook states that there are four Hale elevators to the walkway on the top. That should be a ride itself, since the height is 220 feet. It costs 25 cents a round-trip. Where do we go next?" asked Millicent. "Let's walk down to the east end of the Basin, see where the children's pageant will be held, and have lunch. Is that okay, Mother?"

"I'm ready. I'd also like to see the Lake," she replied enthusiastically.

Elevators to the Top Promenade of Manufactures

#8

Rostral Column Music Hall End of the Peristyle

"What a beautiful walk past the Basin. Lots of people here are having a picnic lunch while they wait for the children's 'Reunion of States' parade," said Millicent, as they stopped before the Music Hall.

The Quadriga Sculpture by Daniel Chester French

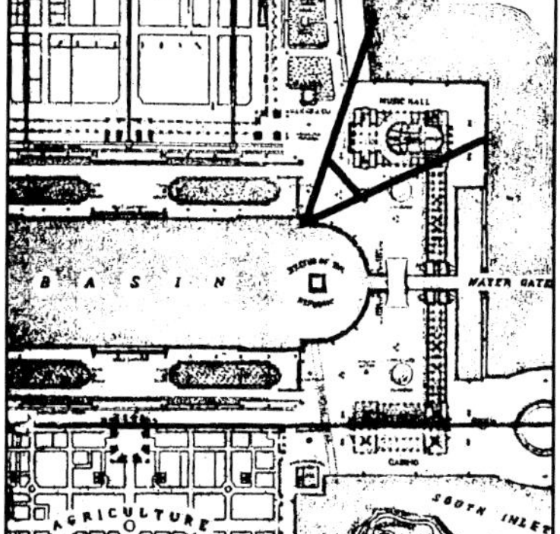

"The guidebook says the Hall is 140 by 200 feet, but the musicians and other statues on top by sculptor Theodore Baur make it look much larger," announced Mother. She added, "The auditorium inside can hold 2000 people."

Millicent remembered, "Its architecture is much like the Casino located at the south end of the Peristyle that we passed on our walk. The restaurant there was packed. Without a doubt, the gilt Quadriga by French showing Columbus driving a four-horse chariot placed at the top and center of the Peristyle was impressive. I want to get a souvenir recipe from the Walter Baker Company for my collection. Their pavilion is right here at the corner of the Manufactures Building. Wait for me."

"While we wait, I'll get a picture of the Music Hall, and one of Jackson Park's six noble and heroic Rostral Columns by Johannes Gelert, which is in front of it," said Harald.

#9

Corner of Manufactures **Music Hall** **Lowney Chocolates** **North Half of the Peristyle**

As they walked away from the Music Hall, they looked back, and Harald noted, "This view gives me the full Rostral Column showing the boat prows, Music Hall, and half the Peristyle's 48 columns—one for each state and territory. I see straight ahead the Lowney chocolate pavilion, modeled after the 'Temple of Vesta.'"

Walter Baker Pavilion

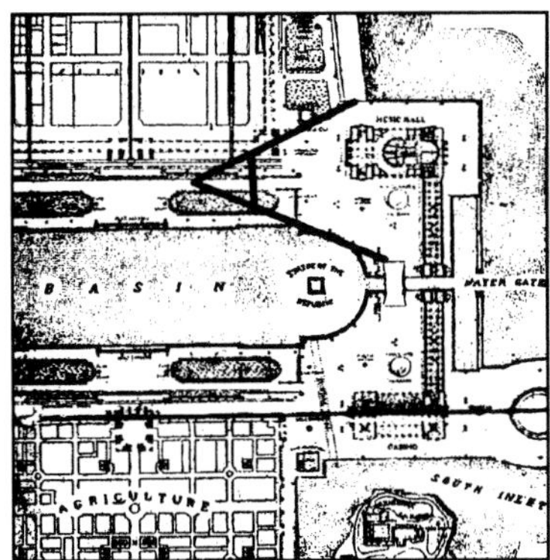

"There is a matching temple at the other end of the Peristyle," said Mother.

Bending over his camera viewfinder, Harald observed, "The crowd is trying to stay off the grass like the signs say, but it's just too inviting a place to spread out a picnic lunch basket."

"Well I'm back," announced Millicent breathlessly as they moved farther along the south face of the Manufactures Building. "I got a souvenir cookbook from Baker by Miss Parloa, and I'm going to try their recipe for chocolate cookies when we get home. They had lots of good baking suggestions. Everything looked scrumptious."

"Let's move around to the west side of Manufactures," said Harald.

CHOCOLATE COOKIES

Beat to a cream half a cupful of butter and one tablespoonful of lard. Gradually beat into this one cupful of sugar; then add one fourth of a teaspoonful of salt, one teaspoonful of cinnamon, and two ounces of W. Baker & Co.'s No. 1 chocolate, melted. Now add one well-beaten egg, and half a teaspoonful of soda dissolved in two tablespoonfuls of milk. Stir in about two cupfuls and a half of flour. Roll thin, and, cutting in round cakes, bake in a rather quick oven. The secret of making good cookies is the use of as little flour as will suffice.

(Walter Baker & Co. *Choice Receipts*)

#10

Gondola on North Canal | Illinois Building | Manufactures Building | Electric Launch

"That was quite a long walk just to get to this corner," gasped Violet.

"But look at this vista! I'd like to have it in color, but that kind of film is just now being developed by the French, or so I've read in my photography magazines," exclaimed Harald.

Venetian Gondola

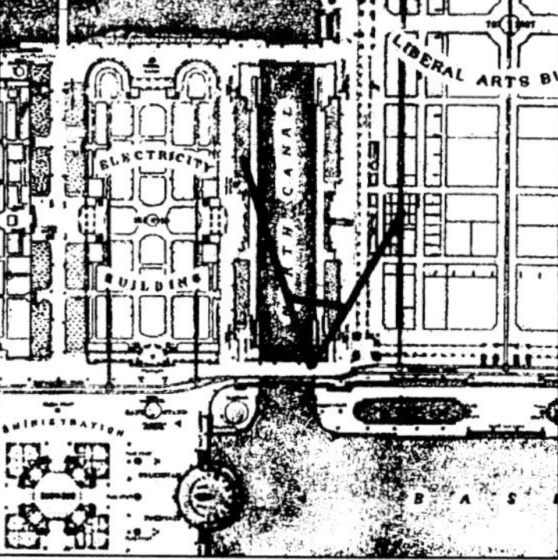

"My, aren't those electric launches with their striped tops pretty," remarked Violet. "There are boat landings all over the park. The boats are full of people today, even the quaint gondolas like the one coming towards us."

"Our map makes me believe that the building way off in the distance at the north end of the Lagoon must be Illinois. Its dome must be very tall to look that big at this distance," mused Millicent with a question in her voice.

"It is. We'll go by it later," answered Harald. He turned to Mother and said, "I heard there are 40 electric launches. I'd like to learn more about the Consolidated Electric Storage Company batteries they use and their General Electric engines."

Millicent pointed up the Canal, "Look, the gondoliers are dressed in bright costumes representing the fourteenth century—this is a Venice for the summer!"

The women agreed when Harald directed, "Let's walk up to the north end of the building."

#11

Part of the German Exhibit in the Manufactures and Liberal Arts Building

"I took only a few indoor pictures yesterday when I got acquainted with the grounds," announced Harald, making conversation as they strolled north past Manufactures. "I don't know if any of them will turn out, because I couldn't judge the light very well. I was looking for the photography exhibit, which they stuck in Classification Group 151 here in the Liberal Arts section. It's upstairs in the gallery. It was fine, except I wish it had been larger. Actually, though, one of the most interesting displays was in the huge German exhibit up there too. I'm reminded of it, since it's right here at the west-center of the building that we're passing now. I took a picture of the bust of Emperor William II atop a pedestal surrounded by greenery and a wreath. I could see the title 'Germany' behind his head. What made the exhibit fascinating for me was the display of lenses and lens-making equipment. They had taken a whole series of photographs using those lenses, and were they stunning! I'd like to get one for my own work."

"Wouldn't that make your camera heavier?" asked Millicent.

"Maybe. It's about four pounds now. Try it out." Harald handed her the camera.

"All I can say is, I'm glad I'm not carrying it around the fairgrounds," she replied, making a face.

"Look at the paintings in the arches in this west entrance: winged allegorical figures of the armorer, brass-worker, iron-worker, and stone mason. There are seated figures representing the decorative arts," explained Mother.

"Those are by Blashfield and Reinhart, respectively," read Millicent from the guidebook. "Up ahead at the northwest corner entrance are paintings by the famous F. D. Millet. Let's take a look."

"Good, I'll look up and try to see the searchlight too," chimed in Harald. "Maybe we can have our lunch."

Searchlight at Northwest Corner of Manufactures

#12

Army Hospital **North Facade of the Manufactures Building**

"Well, so much for hoping for fewer people," remarked Harald, as they rounded the corner and viewed the crowd on the north side of Manufactures. "I do like the imposing facade, though, with the electric lamp poles lined from here to the shore."

"On the left is the porch of the Army Hospital. That facility is adjacent to the Fire Squadron and Guard Station," said Millicent, as she looked at the guidebook map and watched Harald take a picture.

"Mercy sakes, everyone has used this area for a picnic ground! There'll be a cleanup job needed tonight," Mother conjectured.

"Let's join those women picnicking in front of us," suggested Millicent. Harald seconded the idea.

He added, "I'm going to see if they are getting the gas balloon ready for this afternoon's launch."

After finding a place on the cool grass between the Manufactures and Government Buildings, Millicent asked, "Mother, this cold meat dish is excellent and perfect for our outing. May I get the recipe from you?"

"Yes, Dear. I got it from Landis's *World's Fair Recipes*."

Harald returned, announcing that the balloon was being laid out and a big crowd was gathering. He finished his lunch quickly so that they could continue north to the Government Building.

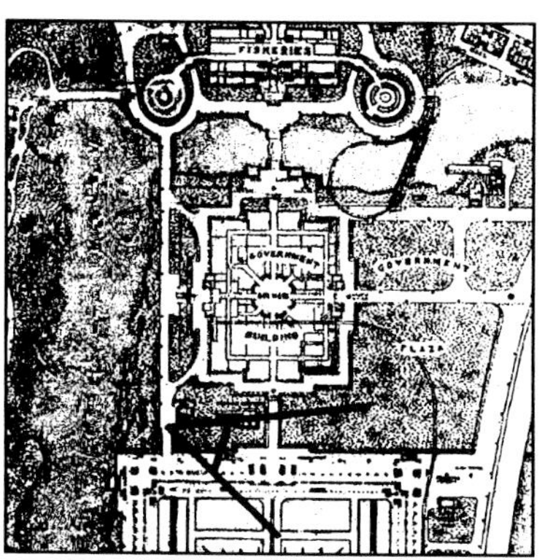

Veal Cake (A Dish for a Picnic).
A few slices of cold roast veal, a few slices of cold ham, two hard boiled eggs, two tablespoonsful[sic] of minced parsley, a little pepper, good gravy, cut off all the brown outside from the veal, and cut the eggs into thin slices, procure a pretty mold, lay veal, ham, eggs and parsley in layers, with a little pepper between each, and when the mold is full get some strong stock and fill up the shape, bake one-half hour and when cold turn it out.

(*World's Fair Recipes* by Jacob Landis)

#13

Fisheries Building   Hygeia Water   West Entrance of the Government Building

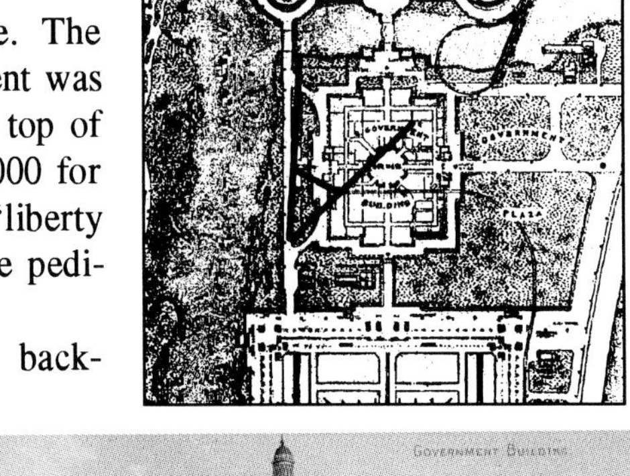

"I'll get a picture of the front of the building. It looks rather 'Governmental,' doesn't it?" questioned Harald.

"Some say the dome is out of proportion to the structure. The guidebook says that W. J. Edbrooke of the Treasury Department was the supervising architect. The size is 350 by 420 feet, and the top of the dome is 275 feet high. The Treasury paid the bill of $400,000 for its construction. This west entrance, which we see here, has a 'liberty group' by A. Waagen and huge bronze eagles surmounting the pediments," Millicent read as a partial answer.

"What's that tent out front—and the building off in the background?" asked Violet.

"The tent is for Hygeia water. There is one on the east side of the building too," replied Harald. "That distant building is Fisheries. Folks are *trying* to stay off the horticulture display here in front of us. I want to walk north and take another picture of the facade to the south, so why don't you try some Hygeia water and send home one of the commemorative chromolithograph postal cards from the post office inside this entrance. Meet me up there when you're finished."

Penny U.S. Postal Card of the Government Building, No. UX10

#14

West Facade of the Government Building **Hygeia Water** **North Facade of Manufactures**

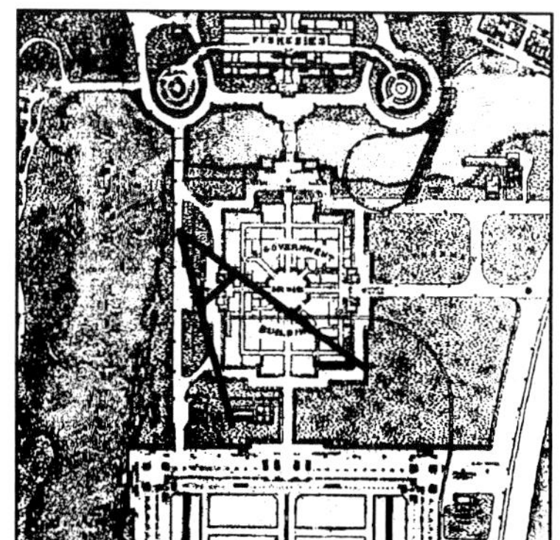

The women disappeared into the Hygeia crowd. "What a huge crowd of spectators around the water pavilion and Manufactures," Harald thought to himself as he gazed at the scene before he took the picture. "And so many more people up on the promenade at the top of Manufactures, especially at the searchlight on the northwest corner. They must be watching the balloon activity on Government Plaza. They also have a perfect view of the beautiful Lagoon behind me and Wooded Island too."

"Oh, here come the ladies," he observed. "Did you mail the card?"

"Yes, and bought you a duplicate for another penny," answered Millicent. "We caught a glimpse of the big redwood trunk exhibit of California under the rotunda, and sneaked a peek at the postage stamp exhibit right by the door."

"I should have had you buy me a set of the Columbian Exposition postage stamps while you were there," mused Harald. "I think they'll be valuable some day."

"What's next?" asked Mother, not at all interested in stamps.

"We'll go around the corner and view the Fisheries Building," said Harald as he picked up his gear and headed north. To himself he thought, "I could really go for a Berghoff* about now."

California Big Tree Exhibit

---

* Berghoff beer, introduced to Chicago at the fair, can still be purchased, especially at the Berghoff Restaurant, Chicago, which is decorated with Exposition pictures.

#15

South Entrance to Fisheries Launches Polygonal Extension on Fisheries Intramural Railroad

Fisheries Arcade

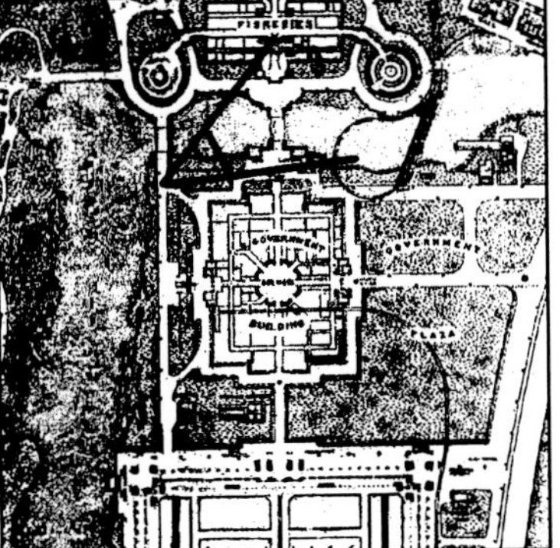

"Isn't this north branch of the Lagoon festive! Look at those loaded electric launches!" exclaimed Mother. "Tell us about the unique Fisheries Building, Millicent."

"Yes," she said, paging through Rand's *Hand Book* to page 143. "The central structure is 162 by 862 feet, and it has two polygonal extensions connected to the main building by curved arcades. One of the extensions is straight ahead, looming up above the bridge between Government and the central Fisheries Building entrance. That makes the ground area about 200 feet wide and 1100 feet long. It's fitting that it has water on two sides." She continued reading, "The architect was Henry Ives Cobb. The cost was $200,000—only half the cost of the Government Building. There are lots of aquaria inside under the towers—both fresh water and salt water. The loggia is just to the left in the view Harald is taking. Look at all the people watching from the bridge."

"I think they may be looking at the north loop of the Intramural Railroad. You can see a bit of it to our right," offered Harald. "Let's get closer by going over the bridge—that railroad is unique."

#16

Intramural Railroad Launch North Facade of the Government Building

As they moved east past the front of Fisheries on the way to the Intramural Railroad, Harald stopped to take a picture of the north side of the Government Building.

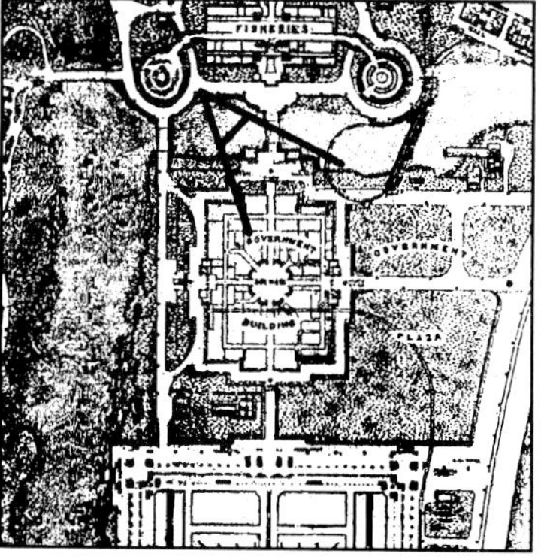

Battleship Illinois Exhibit

"There is a launch pulling up to the boat landing. Lots of folks are waiting for a ride. In fact, there's a solid mass of people on the other side. I can see another tent at the end of the bridge. Is that another Hygeia kiosk?" asked Mother.

"Yes," answered Harald. "They're doing a lively business today. That Government Building facade is massive! The large eagles let you know that it's a national building. I couldn't get it all in my view. I did catch a bit of the elevated train trestle, though."

"Looking in the guidebook, I see that there are several buildings ahead but out of our view. Further on is the Weather Bureau—what a great day they ordered for us! There is also the Life Saving Station, the Lighthouse Exhibit, the Naval Observatory, and on the shore the replica of the battleship 'Illinois.' It has a rock and stone base with wooden sides. But the top has mostly real fittings, so the visitor can get a feel for what life would be like on the real thing."

#17

Launch Under the North Loop of the Intramural Railroad

The trio moved past the entrance of Fisheries to get a closer look at the Intramural Railroad at its north loop.

"Let's wait a minute until the next train turns the loop," said Harald, as he readied the camera on the bridge railing.

Millicent read from the guidebook, "The visitor can now take a trip around the system of the Intramural Elevated Railroad by ascending to a nearby station. The road is 6¼ miles long and was built by the Columbian Intramural Railroad Company at a total cost of $700,000, including power house, rolling-stock, and everything ready for operation. The fare is ten cents for the trip one way or any part of it, and 25 percent of the gross receipts go to the Exposition. The maximum speed is 30 miles an hour." Putting the book down, she exclaimed, "What a great way to get an overview of the grounds and also get around quickly."

"I like the way the electric launches glide right under the trestle," interjected Mother. "They can travel all the way out to Lake Michigan."

"I saw a brochure on the Railroad. They use General Electric motors to run the trains, and the main power station is at the southeast end of the park. It's an exhibit of its own—a favorite of visiting engineers. Using lake water run into the station, they make steam to drive engines that rotate big dynamos which generate the electricity. The electric power is delivered by a true third rail on the trestle contacting a sliding copper spring on each car," explained Harald. "From here you can see part of the ticket and boarding station on the other side of the loop."

"That's very interesting, Dear. Let's try to get something to eat," suggested Millicent. "There are several restaurants on the other side of Fisheries. Let's walk through the building and try one."

#18

Brazil Building **Millicent** **Violet**

"What a good souvenir of the fair I see," thought a contented Harald, as he came out of the Swedish Restaurant after paying the check. "I'll get a picture of that gentleman giving directions to Millicent and Mother. I wonder what they asked him?"

"Wasn't that Swedish food tasty?" Violet was asking Millicent, as Harald finished taking the picture and walked up to them on the avenue.

"Yes. It was a wait, but I got another recipe for my collection. It's from the world's fair souvenir Swedish cookbook, *Hemmets Drottning,*" answered Millicent.

"What directions were you asking?" queried Harald.

Millicent answered, "I wanted to know where the French Building is located since my ancestors came from France. Do we have enough time to go see it?"

"Certainly," he replied. "Before we go, what is that building to the north of us? It was in my camera view."

Millicent paged through the guidebook. "Here it is on page 177, the Brazilian Building. It was designed by Lieutenant-Colonel Francisco de Souza Aguiar, a delegate to the world's fair. It is in the form of a Greek cross, the outside dimensions being 148 by 148 feet. The height is 120 feet. A grand circular staircase leads to a second floor. The cost was $90,000."

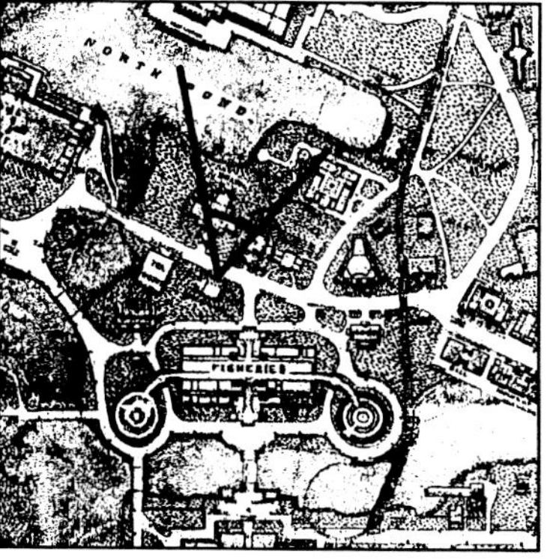

Potatispannkaka (Potato Pancakes)

Fyra stora, kalla, kokta potatis skalas och skäras i bitar; 1 pt. varm mjölk sättes till 2 matskedar mjöl och 2 matskedar smör, salt, peppar och persilja efter behag. Ett lager af denna smet lägges i bottnen på pannan, deröfver ett lager potatis, o. s. v. Till slut slås mjölken öfverst och rifna skorpor sist. Bakas på 15 minuter.

Ellen M. Chandler, World's Fair Lady Manager from Pomfret, Vermont.
(*Hemmets Drottning Kok-Bok*)

#19

They walked up the oval avenue where most of the state and foreign buildings were located. From a distance, they could see the distinctive French Building on the shore of Lake Michigan. It was recognizable by the bold blue, white, and red striped flag fluttering overhead. Clearly, the best vantage point was the broad expanse of open ground near the shore. The northeast breeze was inviting.

As Harald rotated the camera for a vertical view, he asked Millicent, "What are the facts on this stately structure?"

North End of the French Building Taken From the Lakeshore

Finding the description, she read aloud, "There are two pavilions connected by a semicircular colonnade. At the center is a very fine fountain elaborately decorated with bronze statuary brought over from France. This makes a delightful retreat as it faces the lakefront. The architects were Motte & DuBuysson and R. A. Deuelle. The tall one-story exterior in the French Renaissance style is finished in staff. The most popular room is 'De La Fayette,' which contains many gifts, mementos, historical relics, and things of interest regarding the dealings between LaFayette and this country."

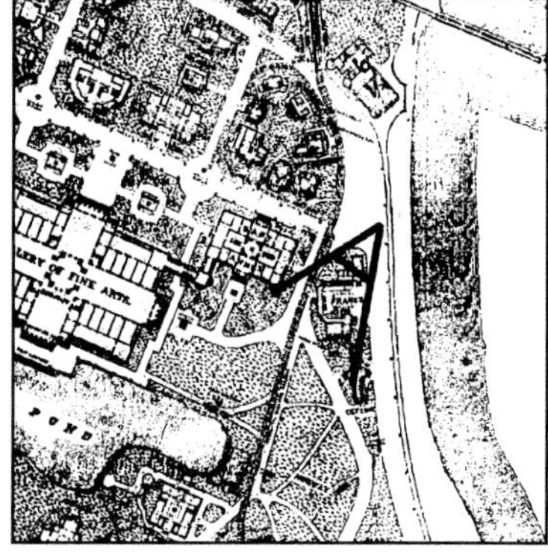

Violet asked, "What is that big unfinished building behind us just outside the park?"

"That's the MacKaye Spectatorium. It was to be the most advanced theater and show arena, but the costs exceeded expectation, and the depression forced a work stoppage. I believe they'll tear it down," explained Harald.

"I guess that's what they call 'bringing down the house,'" quipped Millicent. "Where to next?"

"We'll walk west past the Art Palace toward the Woman's Building," answered Harald.

#20

North Facade of Fine Arts King's Balloon in Front of the Annex Hydrogen Field Generator

"Stop!" called Harald. "I see another balloon and not too many people. I'd like to try and get a picture."

"We'll wait here and admire the front of this magnificent structure," said Millicent, gazing at the Fine Arts Palace.

Harald moved closer to the front and over by the west choragic statue, took a picture, and asked a spectator what was going on.

"Well," asked Millicent as he returned, "what did you learn?"

"The balloon is the *Eagle Eyrie* from Pennsylvania piloted by Sam King of Philadelphia. He and his adventurous crew can get good hydrogen here at the fair. They've apparently had some harrowing flights while here," Harald summarized. "What did you learn about the Fine Arts Building?"

Millicent summarized, too, saying, "C. B. Atwood of Chicago designed this most popular building in the Greek Ionic style. The main building is 300 by 500 feet with two annexes. That's where you— "

Harald interrupted, "The west Annex makes a wonderful shelter for the balloon preparation."

"Each Annex is 120 by 200 feet with connecting galleries to the main building. It's permanent, since it's made out of bricks rather than wood timbers. Halsey C. Ives is the department chief. What treasures he's collected!" continued Millicent.

"You can get to the south entrance by taking a boat up the Lagoon right to the building. What a lovely scene that must make," sighed Mother.

"Let's continue walking toward the Woman's Building," suggested Harald.

Choragic Monument

"You wait here at the Woman's Building to explore it and get a rest," instructed Harald. "I need to take a quick trip into the Midway Plaisance."

#21

Harald Photographed the Algeria and Tunis Exhibit on the Midway

#22

International Dress and Beauty Show on the Midway as Seen by Harald

#23

Northeast Corner of the Woman's Building

"Violet, isn't it inspiring to have a Woman's Building on the grounds?" Millicent asked, as they waited for Harald.

"Yes," she answered. "What did you tell me? —designed by Sophia Hayden of Boston, caryatids modeled by Miss Enid Yandell, figures standing on the roof-line designed by Miss Rideout, interior decorations by Mrs. MacMonnies and Mary Cassat. I thought the library of women authors was very impressive, and the assembly room at the north end where the Board of Lady Managers meet was spacious and beautiful."

"And the women have done so much else at the fair—like the Children's Building next door and the congresses. Of course, I'm glad to see that cooking was featured in the building's model kitchen. I got one of Mrs. Rorer's cookbooks as a souvenir and tasted their sample corn dodgers, which was a favorite pioneer food. I bought a copy of the beautiful cookbook put out by the Board of Lady Managers too," said Millicent, proudly.

"Hello, Harald," the women chimed in unison.

Harald rejoined them and asked, "Did you two have fun? I'll take a picture of the Woman's Building for you."

"Yes, we were just talking about it," answered Millicent. "How about you?"

"Too many enticing things to see and do. I'll have to come back tomorrow with more film. We'd better move along."

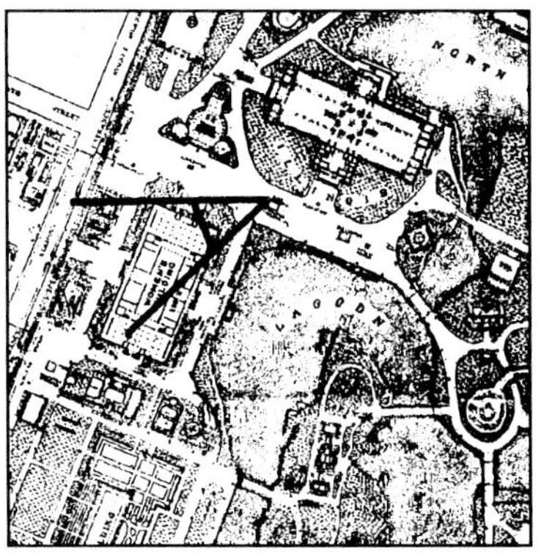

Corn Dodgers

Put 2 cups of white corn meal into a bowl. Pour over it sufficient boiling water to scald, being exceedingly careful to just moisten the meal and to stir all the time. Add to the meal while hot a tablesp. of shortening. When the meal is cool, add one egg beaten until quite light, 2 tablesp. of milk and a teasp. of salt. Mix and bake in a large baking pan by spoonfuls. For instance, put the spoonful down and smooth it until it looks like a small griddle cake. Bake until brown on both sides. These, if properly cooked, make the sweetest of all corn breads.
(Rorer. *Recipes Used in Illinois Corn Exhibit Model Kitchen*)

#24

Hygeia Water Before Merchant Tailor Brazil Sweden Marine Café Fisheries

"The regal look of the front of the Woman's Building is aided by the vista the Lagoon offers," remarked Harald as he prepared to take another picture. "From left to right, I see a familiar Hygeia awning, the Brazil Building, the top of the Swedish Building, the Café de Marine behind the bridge, and, finally, the turrets of the Fisheries Building."

Merchant Tailors' Building

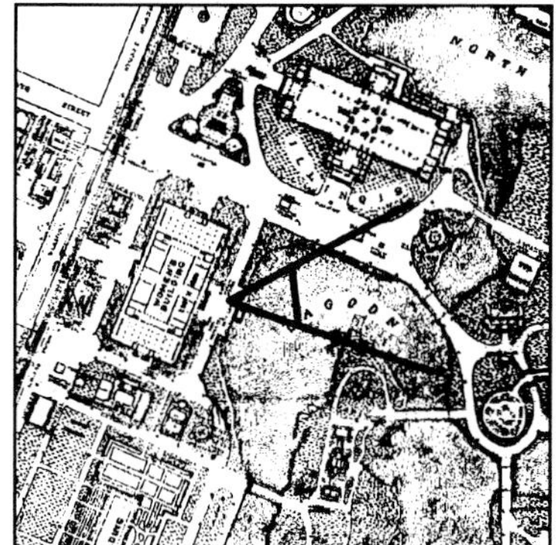

Violet asked, " I can just barely see a building behind the Hygeia stand. What is that?"

Millicent spent a minute consulting the map in the guidebook and reported, "I think that's the Merchant Tailors' Building facing on a bit of the Lagoon."

"The Café, what does it serve? Seafood?"

"Yes," said Harald, moving south to view the Illinois Building.

The Swedish Building

#25

California Building **Illinois Building Decorated for Chicago Day** **Fine Arts Building**

"I could see the Chicago Day decorations on the Illinois Building when we were at the Woman's Building, but this is my first opportunity to get a picture of the whole thing. You know, a person just about needs a camera with interchangeable lenses. Do you see the two cables with the flags of the nations coming down from the dome to the two ends of the building?" asked Harald.

They nodded, and Mother added, "I can also see bunting."

"I wish there were less of a breeze off the Lake so that there'd be a clear reflection of the dome and building in the Lagoon," Harald muttered half to himself while adjusting his camera.

"I can see Fine Arts off to the far right and California Building off to the far left," said Millicent from behind him, while paging for the states section of the guidebook. "Illinois is the largest state building at 160 by 450 feet long and was built in the form of a Greek cross; the short axis is 98 feet wide by 285 long. That little cupola with its beacon on the top of the dome is 234 feet above the ground. That would make the California Building second largest at 144 by 435 feet. I think that's evidence of how they intend to grow in the future. Right now they're promoting the 1894 San Francisco Midwinter Exposition from their building."

"The proportions of the Illinois Building's dome seem too tall and skinny for my tastes," Violet assessed.

"It looks a bit odd," Harald agreed. He added, "But the band music I hear from there tells me they're having a good time today."

"May we detour and take a walk on Wooded Island past the Rose Garden?" asked Mother.

"Sure, maybe we'll see the Japanese Building there too," said Harald.

#26

Fire and Guard Station

Northwest Corner of Manufactures and Liberal Arts Building

Japanese Hoo-den (Temple for the Hoo Bird, or Phoenix)

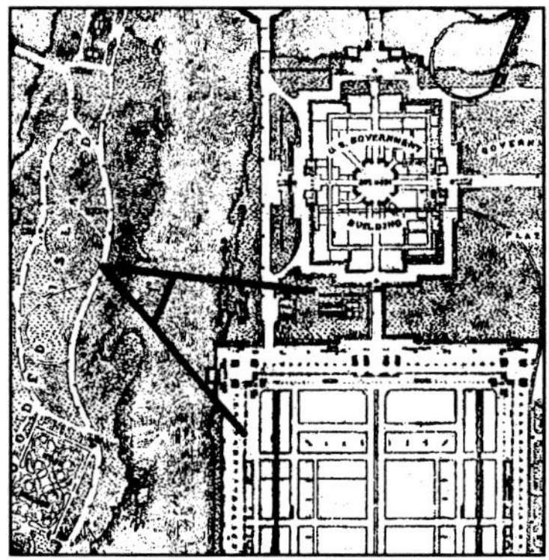

"The Island's foliage has really grown this summer, and the decorations for tonight are all over the place," remarked Violet as they strolled along.

"The guidebook says there are about 2000 varieties of roses in the one-and-a-quarter acre garden. I hope some are still in bloom—it should look grand," voiced Millicent with anticipation.

"As you can see from the picture I'm taking, the Island is a great spot to get views of the major buildings," said Harald. "The Manufactures Building takes up most of my view, but the Fire Squadron and Guard Station Building shows up well too. I know the Columbian guards are busy, but I haven't heard the fire wagons called out since we got here. The station is a large two-story building, which makes you appreciate the immensity of Manufactures."

"Let's take some time to smell the roses," Violet whispered to Millicent.

#27

Tower of Electricity Building **Administration Building** **Mines and Mining Building as Seen From Wooded Island**

"What a pleasant path," said Millicent. "It's like a park within a park. There are exhibits indoors and outdoors. I see plant and shrub varieties from around the world. It looks as though they've had some problems making durable name tags for them, though."

Hunter's (Davy Crockett's) Cabin, Wooded Island

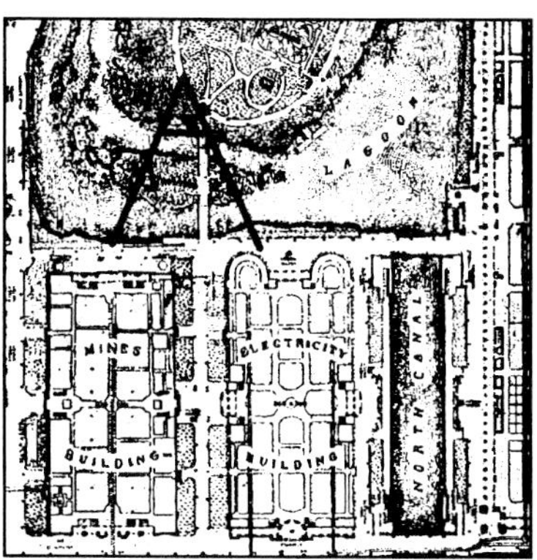

"This is a good view looking south at the Electricity Building, and in the background is Administration," said Harald, taking a photo.

"The guidebook and map show that Hunter's Island is just beyond the trees. On it there's a reproduction of Davy Crockett's log hunting cabin and an Australian Squatter's Hut," said Millicent.

"Millicent, I've been looking through *Favorite Dishes* that you got at the Woman's Building. It's full of interesting ideas by the Lady Managers, who are pictured in it. See, look at this one for Exposition Cake," Violet pointed, as they walked further around the Island.

Exposition Orange Cake

Two cups sugar, two cups of sifted flour, one-half cup of water, two teaspoonfuls yeast powder mixed with the flour, the yolks of five eggs and the whites of three beaten separately, the grating and juice of one orange; bake in layers like jelly cake.

Filling—One cup sugar, grating and juice one orange, whites of two eggs beaten into a froth.

Mrs. S. E. Verdenal, New York Lady Manager
(Shuman. *Favorite Dishes*.)

#28

East Face of Horticulture Building | Illinois Building | Fine Arts | Wooded Island

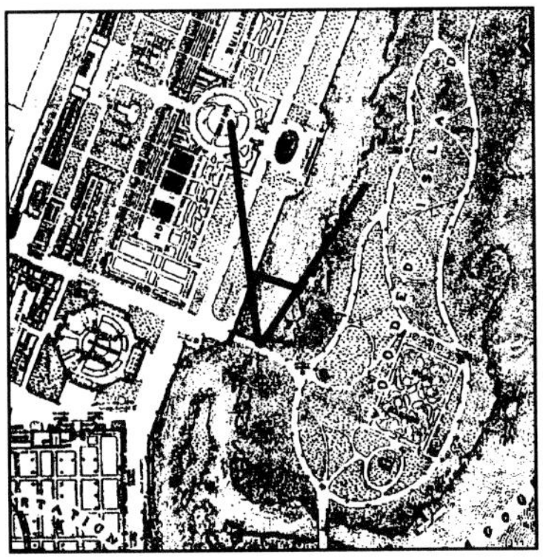

"Can you hear the song of the gondolier?" Millicent asked.

"What a nostalgic view we have of the west Lagoon from this bridge," said Harald, as they emerged from the greenery of Wooded Island. "Now we're at the south end of the Horticulture Building, and the Illinois Building still is imposing even at this distance."

Gondolier in Costume

"I remember canoeing with your father on the lake close to home. This scene reminds me of it. Even though it was years ago, I can still remember everything just as though it were yesterday," Violet reminisced, as she glanced at Harald. "My, how he looks like his father," she thought. Aloud, she added, "My memory is pretty good, although it plays tricks on me at times."

They laughed, and Harald got philosophical, "Your memory is fine. I'm going to use my photographs to remember our trip to the fair. Some take portraits or artistic pictures filled with mood. But I like documentary pictures like Brady took of the Civil War—they're like a historical diary."

"Your enthusiasm for your hobby is contagious. Now, I'd like to see the plants in front of Horticulture," suggested Millicent.

#29

Dome and East Entrance of the Horticulture Building **Illinois Building**

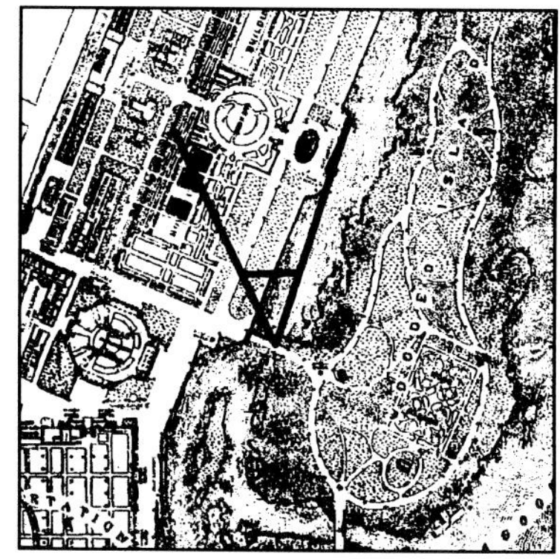

"Look at that full launch. I can hear the laughter from here. This is a good angle, because I can get a large part of Horticulture in my viewfinder," said Harald, as he took another picture from the same spot. "Tell us about the Horticulture Building, Millicent."

"Here's the description. The building was designed by W. L. B. Jenney and W. B. Mundie. My, but it's big! 240 by 1000 feet long, and look at all the glass! It has plants inside, of course, and plants outside also. The glazed glass dome you see is 180 feet in diameter and 114 feet high from its base. The two end pavilions—you can only see one here—are each two stories high, and the second floor fronts are restaurants. How lovely."

"Who designed the statuary?" asked Mother.

"The well-known sculptor, Lorado Taft. The main entrance further up the walk has figures and groups, each of which suggests a botanical theme."

"Who manages all of the exhibits?" asked Harald.

"J. M. Samuels heads this department." Increasingly interested in what she was learning, Millicent added excitedly, "Oh, here's a unique feature: under the dome is a large grouping of palms and ferns on a mound—not too unusual—but under that is a replica of the Mammoth Crystal Cave in the Black Hills of South Dakota. The building is free, but the cave exhibit costs 25 cents."

"Let's take a closer look," suggested Harald. "From here I can see the fine main dome and one of the two smaller entrance domes too."

#30

Saguaro Cactus | "Keep Off The Grass" Sign | Horticulture Building | Illinois Building

Harald captured a picture of Horticulture, making sure the distant dome of Illinois showed.

"Now we can see some of the many plant beds outside. Just imagine what's inside," reflected Millicent, longingly.

"And behind the main building, there are green houses where they force fresh plants. I had to go back there to get my camera permit and saw the Accounting Department, Service Building, and portable Ducker Hospital. Tonight the floats will enter near the south end of Horticulture," said Harald, as he pointed toward the Sixty-second Street gate.

Scene Under the Horticulture Dome

"Look at that weird and ungainly cactus in front of us!" exclaimed Violet. "Those spines look dangerous."

"Apparently the workmen who put up the exhibit knew they were dangerous! See the crowbar marks." agreed Millicent. " The guidebook says you can see lots of cacti on the roof of the Joint Territorial Building—Oklahoma, New Mexico, and Arizona."

"Mind that 'Keep Off The Grass' sign," warned Harald.

#31

Electricity Building Mines Building With Administration in the Background Terminal Station Transportation Building

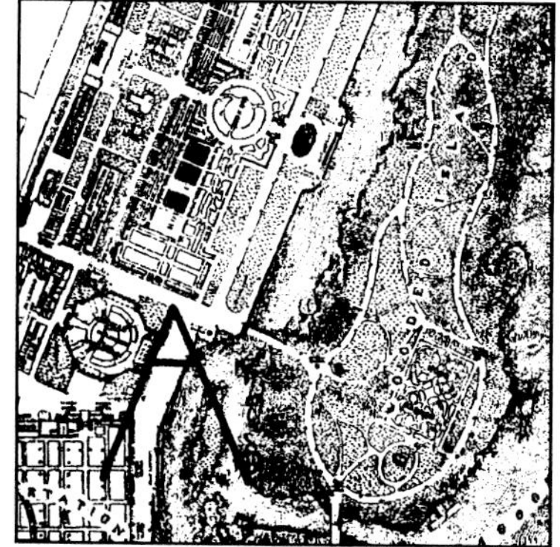

Festival (Choral) Hall to Harald's Right

"This brings us to Festival Hall. Lots of activities are going on here today," said Harald, as they moved along. "From this vantage point, I'm afforded a perspective of Electricity, Mines, and Transportation with Terminal Station in the far background. Say, from this angle, the dome of Administration makes the Mines Building look as if it has a dome."

"The guidebook says Festival Hall next to us is about 250 feet across with rounded corners and is designed in the Doric style. It can hold an audience of 6500 and has several sculptures of famous musicians around the outside," read Millicent.

"Well, this chance to sit a minute feels good," sighed Violet from her seat on the steps.

Millicent spoke softly, "We'd better move along, Harald, so that Mother doesn't get too exhausted."

"Good idea. I'm exhausting my film supply too," he quipped.

#32

Fine Arts Marine Café Fisheries Building Government Wooded Island

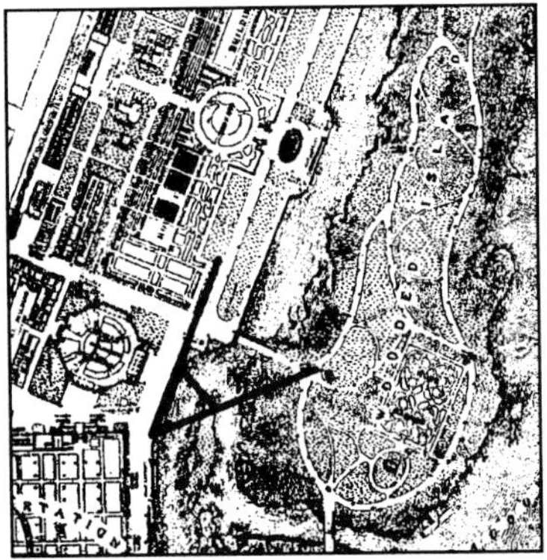

"I like this view. Look at all the people on the bridge! We were there just a few minutes ago," observed Millicent, as they continued south.

"We're a long way from where we were around noon; but you can still get a good view of the Government Building dome on the right, the top of Fisheries, the Marine Café, and a bit of the Fine Arts Palace off to the left," added Harald, as he turned for the picture. He flashed back and said, "Just think, this was scrub brush and marsh two years ago; and now it's scenery, jobs, and ideas. I think we've proven that America can handle big projects. I'm proud to be here and document it."

Fisheries, Millicent's *Hand Book*

"The Transportation Building is behind us. Can you get a picture of it, Son?"

"We're too close. I'll take one for you when we're further away. We're getting near our starting point."

"On our left, we've just passed another Hygeia water pavilion. Does anybody want a drink? I'll go get it," offered Millicent.

The others shook their heads, "No." They moved on.

#33

Manufactures **Electricity Building** **North End of Mines and Mining Building**

"Look at the people gathered here!" exclaimed Mother.

"What a wonderful view of the north sides of Electricity and Mines here on my right," said Harald, as he climbed up on the stairs at the side of the entrance to Transportation to get above the crowd. "Well, it's not a perfect view of the architecture with that electric light in front of me. But that's okay, it's part of the show."

Wisconsin Exhibit in the Mines Building

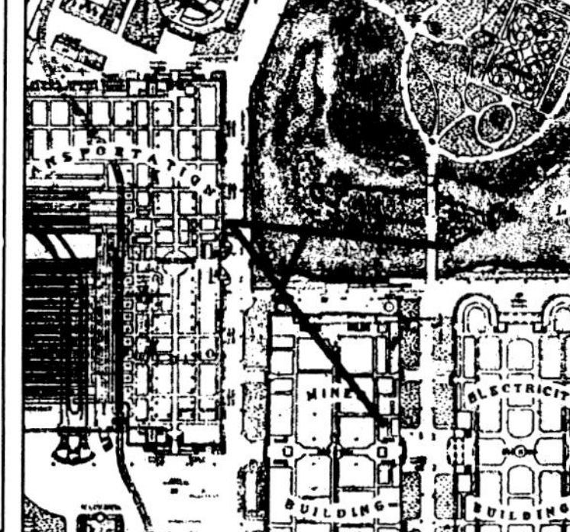

"The guidebook says Henry Van Brunt & Howe of Kansas City designed the Electricity Building, and John Barrett is chief," announced Millicent. "What is fascinating is the advance of technology. Bell's telephone was used to make a long distance call from Philadelphia to Washington at the 1876 Centennial fair, and here they made a long distance call from Chicago to the East Coast! I read in the paper that Elisha Gray is active here too. Do you remember he lost the telephone patent to Bell? The paper said that Gray invented the coin-operated phone."

"What is that illustration in the guidebook?" asked Mother.

"It's the Wisconsin exhibit in Mines," replied Millicent. "The huge sandstone monoliths at each corner came from their famous quarries."

#34

Transportation Building Choral Hall South End of Horticulture

"In this view I'll get about half of Transportation, the fine front of Choral Hall and the south pavilion and dome of Horticulture," said Harald, as they stopped momentarily by the Mines and Mining Building at the south end of the Lagoon.

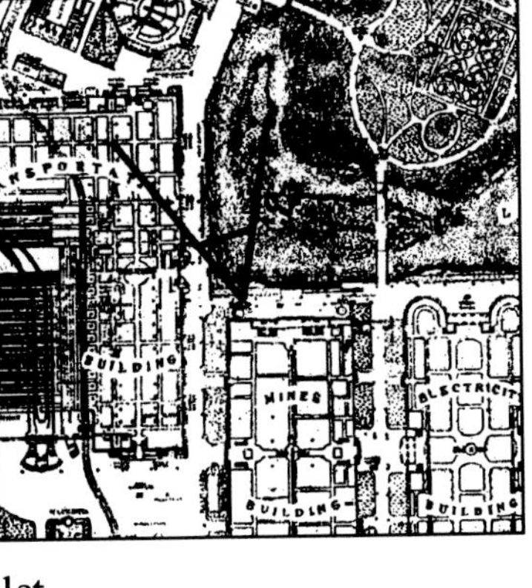

"What's that two-masted boat in front of us?" asked Violet.

"I've seen it moored in the same spot in pictures of the fair, but I don't know its purpose," answered Harald.

Millicent proceeded to find information on the Transportation Building in the guidebook. "See how dark the facade is? Louis Sullivan and Dankmar Adler of Chicago were the architects, and they didn't use white to spray-coat the $370,000 building. Willard Smith is chief of this huge 256- by 960-foot building. Imagine, the attached Annex doubles that area. There are several separate but related corporate buildings, like the Pennsylvania Railroad."

"Golden Entrance" to the Transportation Building Illustrated on the Cover of Millicent's Guidebook

#35

Illinois Building — Soda Water Stand — West Face of Manufactures — Ticket Booth

"Wait here a minute while I cross the bridge over to Manufactures to get a picture of those spectators at the boat landing," came the request from Harald, as they got to North Canal.

"Be quick, please," replied Millicent. The two women stood at the corner and watched the people go by. Soon, a young man came by handing out pamphlets. They walked over and found out that he was distributing flyers from the American Biscuit Manufacturing Company exhibit over in the Agriculture Building.

"Thank you," said Millicent, taking one eagerly.

"My land, these are recipes. And by Mrs. Rorer too!" noticed Mother, looking over her daughter-in-law's shoulder.

"They're all different from the recipes I got at the Woman's Building," said Millicent as she paged through the pamphlet. The Cracker Croquettes recipe on page two sounds interesting."

Harald returned in time to agree with her. "The folks are thick over there, many resting. The enthusiasm of this morning has dwindled somewhat, but the scene is still festive. The steps down to the water visually connect the water to the buildings so well. The lengthening shadows should make for a crisp picture. I think the soda water kiosk there provides a perfect beverage at a boat landing."

"Let's head slowly down toward Agriculture," said Millicent, concerned about Violet's strength after their long walk.

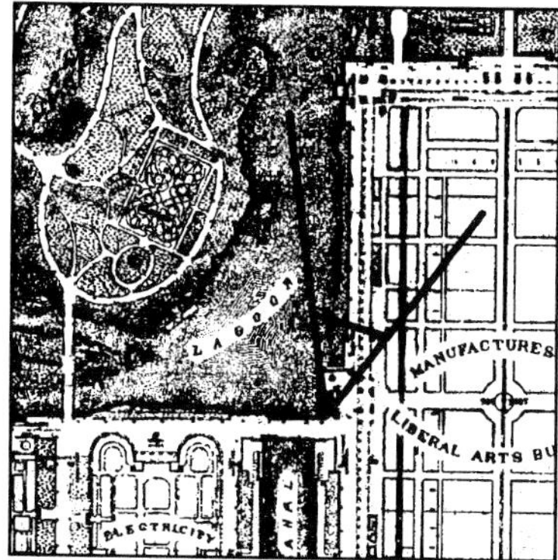

Cracker Croquettes.

To one pint of rolled Soda Crackers or Saratoga Flakes allow half pint of milk, yolks of two eggs, grated rind of one lemon, quarter cup sugar. Put crumbs and milk over fire; when hot add all the other ingredients. Cook a minute and turn out to cool. When cold, form into pyramids, dip in beaten egg and then in dry crumbs, and fry in smoking hot fat. Serve with a pudding sauce, as a sweet entrée.

(Rorer. *Some Dainty Ways for Serving Crackers.*)

#36

West Entrance of the Manufactures and Liberal Arts Building

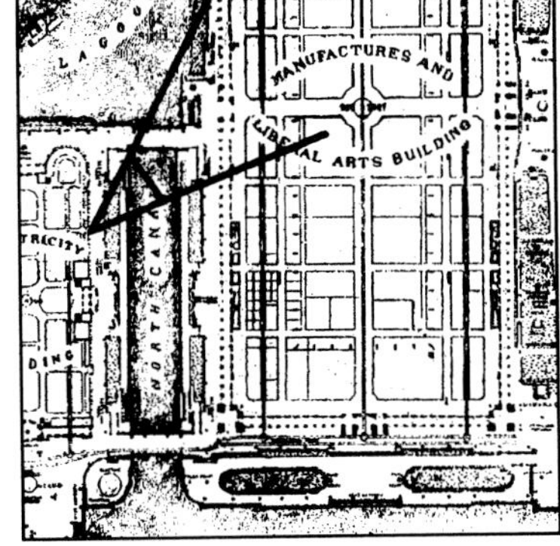

"Remember when we passed Manufactures? Now I can get a picture of this west entrance and the bridge across the North Canal," yelled Harald down to the ladies from his higher position at the Electricity Building.

"I'll guess that the Electricity Building is all aglow in the evenings," Mother exclaimed, gazing at it with wonder.

"There are thousands of arc and incandescent lights inside and outside at the fair," offered Millicent. "It's the trademark of the Exposition. I venture to guess that all homes will be lit with electricity some day. It's so much safer and more convenient than gas. Why, they're even cooking with electricity in homes now!"

"I caught a glimpse of the tribute to Edison in Electricity," remarked Harald, upon his return. "It has 5000 red, white, and blue bulbs spiraling up to a giant cut-glass replica of a light bulb at the top. It's a light show that can't be surpassed!"

"Let's move down further along Electricity to the big east entrance," suggested Millicent.

82 Foot Tall Edison "Tower of Light" by General Electric in the Electricity Building

#37

Manufactures Building **North Canal** **Agriculture Building** **Colonnade in Distance** **Electricity**

"Four Races" by Martiny

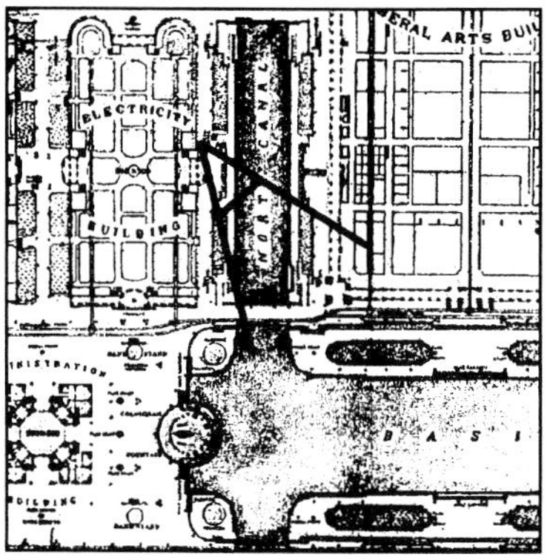

"This quarter-point entrance at Electricity gives me a chance to view the Agriculture Building, North Canal, and part of South Canal with its Colonnade in the distance," described Harald, as he talked more to his camera than to the ladies.

"Please tell me about the Agriculture Building, Millicent," requested Mother.

"It's in the shape of a stout 'T' with the top bar being 500 by 800 feet. The base, which is called the Annex, is about half that size. The main statuary is by Philip Martiny of Philadelphia. He did the 'Four Races' above one of the four corners. The statue on the dome near the center—you can just see it from here—is called 'Diana' by Augustus Saint-Gaudens. He first designed a Diana for the new Madison Square Garden in New York and also designed the official Exposition award medal. George Maynard painted the interior decorations. McKim, Meade, and the flamboyant Stanford White of New York were the architects."

"Come on, Kodak fiend, let's move closer," chided Millicent, as Harald walked up.

#38

Manufactures Casino Rostral Column Agriculture Building Proctor's Polar Bear

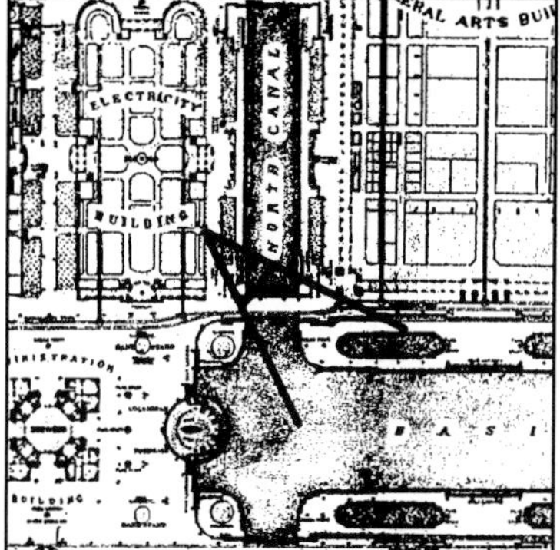

"I can get a good snapshot of Agriculture from the other quarter-point entrance of Electricity," explained Harald, as he rushed away to get the picture.

"Did you get the entire Basin?" asked Millicent when he returned.

"Yes," came the answer followed by more details. "The Casino is on the left down at the end. It's a good complement to the scene."

"The guidebook says it is 140 by 246 feet—just like Music Hall we saw earlier—and three stories high. The Bureau of Public Comfort runs the coat and bag check and has lavatories on the first floor. The entire second floor is a public restaurant seating 1500."

"Are those animal sculptures?" asked Violet, peering at the bridge.

"Yes, in fact, they are our native animals that many have not seen in the wild," read Millicent from page 81. "They were sculpted by Edward Kemeys and A. Phimister Proctor. Nearest us on the end of the bridge I can see the two Polar Bears suggesting the most recent Arctic explorations."

"I can get better views of the entire Court from the front portico of Electricity. We can get there by going up these stairs to the bridge," encouraged Harald.

"I'd like to head home soon, Son," voiced Violet.

"All right. I'm about finished too," answered Harald.

"Polar Bear" by Proctor

#39

Southwest Corner of Manufactures

Statue of the Republic in the Distance Before the Peristyle

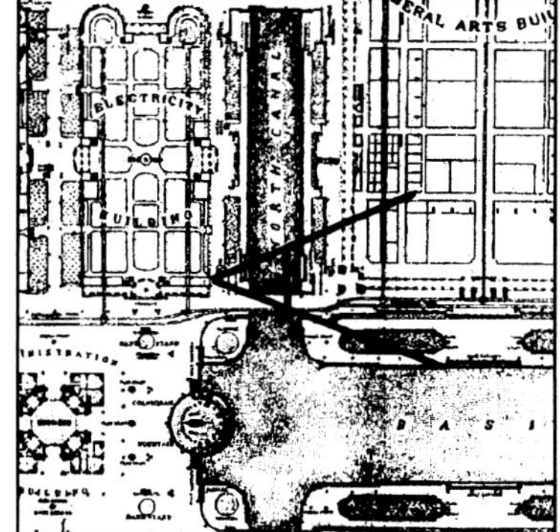

"That balcony on Electricity was a great place to take pictures," Harald announced exuberantly, returning to the women seated on the steps. "I took several to form a sort of panorama. The first will show the entire southwest entrance to Manufactures. I think I had a good view in the foreground of one of Proctor's Polar Bears. Off in the distance at the east end of the Basin I could see the gilt Statue of the Republic. What does *Rand* say about it?"

Millicent checked the index in the back of the book and turned to page 111. "The statue[*] by Daniel Chester French is 65 feet high and stands on a stout base 35 feet high. She wears a formal Grecian robe and has on her head a laurel wreath illuminated with 13 lamps. Her left arm holds a staff carrying the symbol of liberty—the Phrygian cap, and a globe surmounted by an eagle is in her other hand. Good! The guidebook gives some sizes so we can judge how colossal she is: the distance between her chin and the top of her head is 15 feet, and her arms are 30 feet long! Her head alone weighs one and a half tons. Imagine gilding all that!"

Harald added, "The Columbus Arch under the Quadriga on the Peristyle is visible, too, along with a full Rostral Column with Neptune and his trident on top. Come to think of it, there is a theme of exploration by sea here: Columbus rides in a chariot from the ersatz ocean—Lake Michigan, MacMonnies' fountain, Rostral Columns, and the amazing and beautiful Viking ship[**] that was built in Norway and sailed in the old-fashioned way to Chicago just to be exhibited at the fair."

---

[*] See page 9 for a detailed view. French is known for his seated Lincoln in the Memorial at Washington, D.C.

[**] The Viking ship, which survives today, was moored on the lakeshore near the battleship Illinois exhibit.

#40

Electricity Building Fisheries and Fine Arts West Face of Manufactures Building North Canal

"I also took a view up the North Canal into the Lagoon. This gave me the long sweep of giant Manufactures—that's where the dedication ceremonies were held less than a year ago."

"You seem to be taking a lot of pictures of Manufactures," said Millicent.

U.S. Pavilion in Manufactures

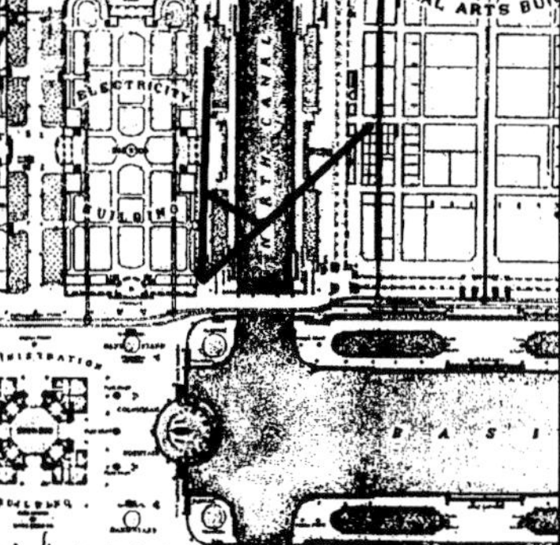

"Well, you're right," Harald agreed. "It's captured my imagination, because it's a record-breaking engineering fete. It has a kingdom of artifacts, products, and learning under one roof. Men died just putting it up. With its Wellington Catering Restaurants and other facilities, it's a small city here in Chicago. I guess it's fitting that the Yerkes telescope* with the world's largest objective lens should be nestled within it. What an instrument! The photographs they'll make with it will open up new understanding about the universe."

Looking in her guidebook, Millicent remarked, "Another national entry I see illustrated here is the grand U.S. Pavilion on the main floor."

---

* The telescope is still in operation at Lake Geneva, Wisconsin. Charles T. Yerkes, Chicago City Railway magnate, was a director of the World's Columbian Exposition.

#41

Manufactures **Lowney Chocolates** **Statue of the Republic** **Casino** **Agriculture**

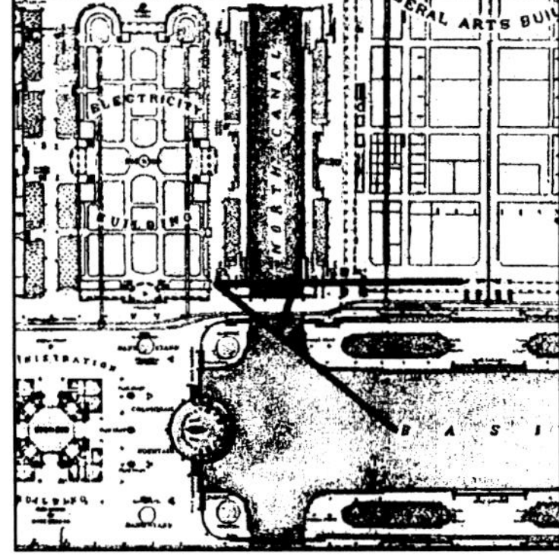

"I noticed that you moved a little farther south. What did you see?" came Millicent's next question.

"A better view of the Basin and all of its sights—better balance I think, especially the broad expanse of the Peristyle. You could just see the Casino Pier through the rows of columns. The *Rand* guide?"

"The Pier is a half-mile long and 400 feet wide with berths on each side for boats of all types and ticket entrances on both sides as well. There is an anchorage for yachts about 200 feet beyond the end of the Pier. The water is 15 to 18 feet deep at the Pier's far end, so larger ferries like the *Christopher Columbus* can navigate safely. The World's Fair Steam Launch Company runs ferry boats from the Clam Bake Restaurant to the Pier to South Pond and back—a fast way to go from the north end of the park to the south end. To aid passengers, there is a Movable Sidewalk concession extending the length of the Pier. The popular ride is the first of its kind. You move slowly on the outside loop and faster on the inside loop. Even if you're not coming or going by boat, the Lake air out there is refreshing."

Casino Pier and Moveable Sidewalk From the Top of the Peristyle

#42

Harald continued to explain his panorama: "I turned my camera south for a new scene. In the center was Cleopatra's Needle obelisk at the end of South Canal. Behind it was the Colonnade; and behind its columns, I could just see the Stock Pavilion where lots of activities are taking place today. In front of me was one of the electric fountains, and on the right, MacMonnies. I hadn't snapped Machinery Hall before. What do we know about Machinery, Millicent?" asked Harald.

Agriculture Electric Fountain Colonnade Behind Obelisk MacMonnies Before Machinery

"Machinery Hall is 850 by 500 feet with an Annex 550 by 490 feet, not including the Power House, the total costing $1,200,000. Peabody and Stearns of Boston were the architects, and they used a Spanish Renaissance style. L. W. Robinson is chief. A wonderful 50-foot-wide gallery runs along the north and east sides and affords broad vistas of the Court of Honor. Six large figures at the entrance and most of the other decorations were sculpted by M. A. Waagen."

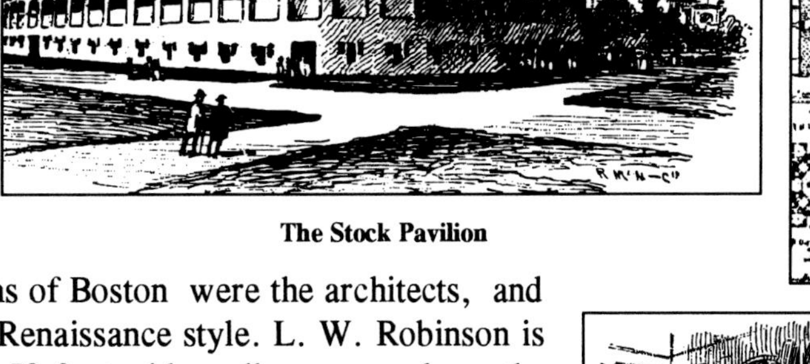

The Stock Pavilion

"Oh, you youngsters, I'm more tired than my feet—if that's possible. Can we take the "L" or train home?" sighed Mother.

"You've been a trooper," declared Harald, with Millicent nodding assent. "How about going over to the Pier instead and taking a boat ride home? It would be the same distance and a new experience."

"What a fun idea," agreed the two women.

Dynamo and Switchboard in Machinery

#43

North Entrance of Agriculture From Across the Basin

"My, Agriculture is commanding when backlit by the setting sun!" exclaimed Violet, as they viewed the building from across the water.

"Yes, and look at all the people around the Basin! They're finding choice spots to view the Night Pageant," surmised Harald. "Going this way we'll see the setup for tonight's fireworks at the Lake."

"Now you can see the Diana statue that graces the top of the dome," Millicent pointed out. "And look at the two heroic sculptures on either side of the entrance."

"Thank you both for a most wonderful day!" Mother said sincerely. "Pshaw, so many sights! I'm overwhelmed. And the celebration— Everybody wants to know the attendance today!"

"You're so very welcome, Violet. You've been excellent company on this adventure," returned Millicent, and Harald nodded approval.

"Ladies, I have a very small gift for you both for being so patient with my photography. I went into the Midway to get you souvenirs. I didn't know what and didn't have much time, so after taking a picture of the Algeria and Tunisia exhibit, I stopped at the neighboring Vienna Model Bakery and got two souvenir cookbooks which feature Bensdorp products served there."

"What a wonderful surprise!" smiled Millicent, paging through her book. "Let's go, home, and I'll make you some of their ice cream!"

Harald offered his arms and escorted the women to the boat.

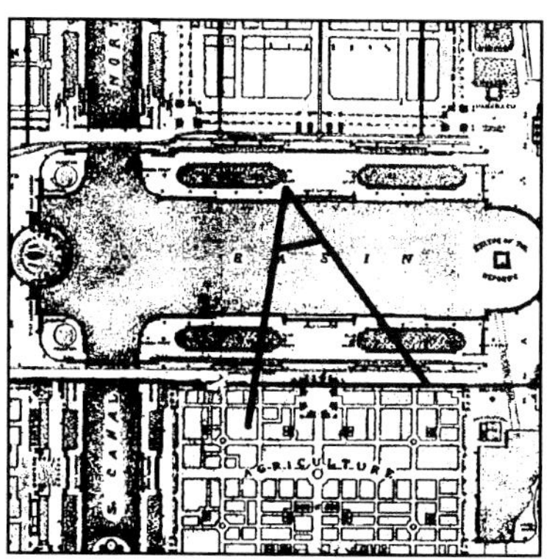

Cocoa Ice Cream

Scald 1 pint milk; beat 3 eggs till light; mix 3 tablespoonfuls sugar, a pinch of salt, and 2 teaspoonfuls **Bensdorp's Royal Dutch Cocoa;** add it to the beaten eggs, and when well mixed pour on slowly the hot milk; turn back into the double boiler and cook until it thickens like soft custard, stirring constantly; when smooth add 1 cup sweet cream and 1 tablespoonful sugar, or enough to make it quite sweet, stir until the sugar is dissolved, then strain through a finer strainer; when cool add 1 tablespoonful vanilla, and freeze the same as any ice cream.

(Bensdorp. *A Few Choice Cooking Recipes.*)

The End

ILLUSTRATED REFERENCE LIST

Aeronautics. M. N. Forney, ed. New York: American Engineer and Railroad Journal. Vol. 1, No. 1, 1893, and Vol. 1, No. 8, 1894. This publication commenced with the first Congress of Aeronautics, which was held at the Columbian Exposition, and is the proceedings of the Congress. Contains information on King's flight from the Art Palace in the "Eagle Eyrie" and the Signal Corp's "General Myer" from Government Plaza.

Bancroft, Hubert Howe. *The Book of the Fair : an Historical and Descriptive Presentation of the World's Science, Art, and Industry, as viewed through the Columbian Exposition at Chicago in 1893.* 2 vol. Chicago: Bancroft, 1893. 1 *l*, 1000 p. continuously paged. A major history of the fair. Chicago Day is described from pages 808-10. The German section of Liberal Arts is described on page 239, and a picture of part of that exhibit nearly identical to HRP's image #11 is illustrated. George Ferris portrait; choragic monuments at Fine Arts, pages 666-67.

[Banks, Charles Eugene]. *The Artistic Guide to Chicago and the World's Columbian Exposition.* [Chicago]: Columbian Art, 1892. 421 p., hardcover. Good description of city services, amenities, and the theater district.

Bensdorp & Company. *A few choice cooking receipts for the use of Bensdorp's Royal Dutch Cocoa.* [Boston]: Stephen L. Bartlett, 1893? 16 p., wraps, cover title. Gives fair locations that used Bensdorp cocoa, including the Vienna Bakery on page 15. Recipes by Mrs. D. A. Lincoln, author of the *Boston Cook Book.*

A Biographical History with Portraits of Prominent Men of the Great West. Chicago: Manhattan Publishing, 1894. William R. Kerr biography on page 199.

Brown, Julie K. *Contesting Images : Photography and the World's Columbian Exposition.* Tucson: U of Arizona P, [©1994]. xvi, 185 p. Extensive description and analysis of the various photographic displays and concessions at the fair, including amateur photography. Illustrated.

Bullard, Thomas R. *The Columbian Intramural Railway: A Pioneer Elevated Line.* Oak Park, IL: [Thomas R. Bullard], 1987. 19 p., illustrated, wraps. An excellent description of the Intramural, including the technology used.

COLUMBIAN
INTRAMURAL
RAILWAY

BY

Thomas R. Bullard

Cameron, William E[velyn], ed. *History of the World's Columbian Exposition.* 2nd ed. Chicago: Columbian History, 1893. 356, (6) p. Illustration of Montgolfier statue in the Transportation Building.

Cameron, William E[velyn]. *The World's Fair, Being A Pictorial History of The Columbian Exposition.* Reading, PA: J. I. Mattes, [©1893 by J. R. Jones]. 3 *l*, 816 p., hardcover. A general history of the fair. Portraits of M. P. Handy and General Miles.

Campbell, J. B. *World's Columbian Exposition Illustrated.* Vol. 3. Chicago: Campbell, 1893. A monthly illustrated magazine devoted to the world's fair. Illustration of "Old Glory" balloon from July 4, Tucker portrait, Chicago Day on the Plaza, Elgin Band, Mexican Band, ringing of New Liberty Bell, Plaza scene in evening, and the International Rope.

Carlton, W. F. *The Amateur Photographer : A Complete Guide for Beginners in the Art-Science of Photography.* 12th ed. revised. Rochester, NY: [Rochester Optical], 1894. 64 p., wraps. "price 25 cents." Handy guide of the day for amateurs.

Chicago Daily News. September 23 to October 12, 1893. Chicago newspaper with descriptions of Chicago Day planning and the event. Grand Cloak ad for Chicago Day and cut of William Kerr.

Chicago Herald. September 19 to October 12, 1893. Descriptions of Chicago Day planning and the event. Cuts of cannon start, buglers' costumes, trampling of the grass, Fair department store ad, *Inter Ocean* ad; Chicago Day special issue.

Chicago Tribune. August 14 to October 12, 1893. Descriptions of Chicago Day planning and the event. Cut of "Elestra," cartoon of St. Louis withholding floats, planned parade route, and cut of the Isabella float.

City of Chicago. Pratt, S[ilas] G[amaliel], ed. *Official Souvenir Program of Chicago Day at the Fair*. Chicago: Knapp, 1893. (34) p., color wraps (illustrated on front cover). On Title page: "Wm. R. Kerr, Chairman of the Committee. Edited by S. G. Pratt, Projector and Director of the Program. Price 25 cents." Plan of Chicago Day, line drawings of the floats.

Dybwad, G[ay] L[eon], and Joy V[ernelle] Bliss. *Annotated Bibliography: World's Columbian Exposition, Chicago 1893*. Albuquerque, NM: The Book Stops Here, 1992. 1 *l*, xii, 444, (2) p. plus tipped-in folding map and Exposition organization chart, softbound. Contains over 2700 citations on all subjects including Federal and state statutes, music, salesman's samples, World's Congresses, and recent books about the Columbian Exposition.

Glimpses of the World's Fair : A Selection of Gems of the White City seen Through a Camera. Chicago: Laird & Lee, 1893. 97 *l* of plates; reprinted many times in hardcover and wraps. On verso of title page: "All pictures in this book were taken with a No. 4 Kodak." Illustrations of the Administration Building, Art Palace, Ferris Wheel, MacMonnies Fountain, and captive balloon on the Midway.

The Graphic. Chicago: Graphic. 9 (1893). An illustrated news magazine. Article on Kiralfy and his spectacle, *America*; hand camera permit illustration.

The Graphic History of the Fair. Chicago: Graphic, [©1894]. 239, (1) p., hard cover. Illustrations of the balloon ascension of Baldwin on Chicago Day and Horace Tucker.

Hannon, Daniel Leroy. *The MacKaye Spectatorium : A Reconstruction and Analysis of a Theatrical Spectacle Planned for the World's Columbian Exposition of 1893*. Ph.D. Diss. Tulane U, 1970. Ann Arbor: UMI, ©1971. x, 320 *l*. A complete description of this grand enterprise that failed.

Harper's Weekly. New York: Harper. 37 (1893). Illustration of Chicago Day night illumination by Graham and float by Butler. Portrait of Bonney and illustration of the viaduct on the Fourth of July.

Hemmets Drottning : Verldsutställningens Souvenir Kokbok. Chicago: Fort Dearborn Publishing, [©1893, ©1894]. 604 p., hardcover with illustration of the Administration Building. Contains numerous recipes in Swedish as offered by various members of state and national boards of lady managers to the world's fair. An English language edition was also printed.

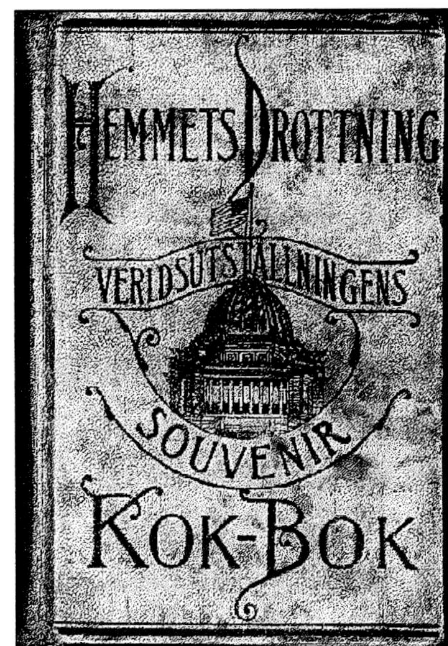

Illustrated American. New York: Illustrated American. 14 (1893). Description of Emma Sickles' stand on Indian rights and the Government's response.

Image. Rochester, NY: George Eastman. 39.1-2 (1996): 1-27. Extensive and detailed account of Kodak at the Columbian Exposition by Julie K. Brown titled "'Seeing and Remembering': George Eastman and the World's Columbian Exposition."

Inter Ocean. Chicago newspaper. 1893. Color cover for October 9 Chicago Day special morning issue (illustrated on page 3). "The Exposition Out of Debt" from the October 9 "Illustrated Supplement," originally in color (illustrated on page 41).

Jamestown Daily Alert. Jamestown, ND. Detailed article about Chicago Day. October 10, 1893.

Janesville Gazette. Janesville, WI. The front page of the newspaper of October 10, 1893, devoted to Chicago Day.

Jenks, Tudor. *The Century World's Fair Book for Boys and Girls*. New York: Century, [©1893]. xiii, 246 p., hard cover. Excellent illustrated description of the beginnings and sights at the Exposition based on Jenks' attendance. Through the fictional Harry and Philip, their tutor (Jenks) takes them through the fair. Early in the fair, the price for a camera permit was $2 a day; later, after protests, the fee was $5 a week (page 141); and according to the story, the permit was rarely requested by fair officials or ticket-takers (page 141). Many references to photography of the day throughout.

Johnson, William Fletcher, and John Habberton. *"My Country, 'Tis of Thee!" : or, The United States of America; Past, Present and Future*. Philadelphia: International, 1892. 3 *l*, 611 p. Portraits of Thomas W. Palmer, Bertha Palmer, Harlow N. Higinbotham, and Moses P. Handy.

Landis, Jacob F. *World's Fair Recipes*. Allentown, PA?: Landis, [c1893]. 118 p., caption title. Also contains recipes for folk curatives.

Lowe, David. *Lost Chicago*. New York: American Legacy, [c1975, c1985]. xii, 1 *l*, 241 p., hardcover. Describes old Chicago and structures lost to the wrecking ball and calamity. Includes reasons for the 1871 fire, the Columbian Exposition, railroad depots, and the White City amusement park.

McShane, Linda. *"When I Wanted the Sun to Shine" : Kilburn and Other Littleton, New Hampshire Stereographers*. [Littleton: McShane, c1993]. vi, 121 p., softbound. B. W. Kilburn was the largest stereoscopic view card maker. Owner Benjamin Kilburn had secured the exclusive rights for taking and selling stereos of the Columbian Exposition. He photographed the fair on several trips including Chicago Day. Kilburn stereo views from October 9, 1893, are numbered 8460 to 8479 and 8781.

Mortimer, F. J. *Wall's Dictionary of Photography*. Boston: American Photographic, [c1943]. Revised by A. L. M. Sowerby. A reference guide for amateur and professional photographers. The platinum paper sensitizing and printing processes span pages 511-515.

The National Cyclopædia of American Biography : Being the History of the United States. Vol. 10. Ann Arbor: UMI, 1967. Biography and illustration of Silas Gamaliel Pratt on page 196.

Neely's Photographs : Chicago Minneapolis St. Paul. New York: Neely, [ca. 1895]. (160) p. of plates, hardcover. Illustration of the Art Institute and whaleback boat.

Northrop, H[enry] D[avenport]. *The World's Fair As Seen In One Hundred Days*. Philadelphia: National, [c1893]. xxii, 720 p., illustrated hardcover. A general history of the fair. Cut of the Japanese Hoo-den.

Parloa, Maria. *Choice Receipts : Specially Prepared for Walter Baker & Co's Exhibit at the World's Columbian Exposition 1893*. Dorchester, MA: Baker, c1893. 32 p., cover title. Recipe booklet.

Pictorial Album and History : World's Fair and Midway. [Chicago: Harry T. Smith], n. d. (288) p. Portraits of the fastest ticket men, Decker and Jones.

Rand, McNally & Company. *Rand, McNally & Co.'s A Week at the Fair : Illustrating the Exhibits and Wonders of the World's Columbian Exposition*. Chicago: Rand, 1893. 268 p. A very useful reference; contains a card map of Chicago and Columbian Exposition and wood cuts of exhibits.

Rand, McNally & Company. *Rand, McNally & Co.'s Handbook of the World's Columbian Exposition*. Chicago: Rand, 1893. 224 p., colored wraps. Authors' copy found with purple stamp from the World's Fair Novelty Stand (reproduced on page 90). Wood cut illustrations.

Rorer, Sarah T. *Recipes Used in Illinois Corn Exhibit Model Kitchen : Woman's Building Columbian Exposition : Chicago 1893*. Chicago?: Illinois Women's Exposition Board, 1893. 16 p., cover title.

Rorer, Sarah T. *Some Dainty Ways for Serving Crackers*. Chicago?: American Biscuit Manufacturing, c1893. (8) p., wraps, cover title. Over stamp in purple. A recipe booklet handout at the Exposition.

World's Columbian Commission. Board of Lady Managers. Shuman, Carrie V., comp. *Favorite Dishes : A Columbian Autograph Souvenir Cookery Book.* Chicago: Shuman, 1893. 221 p., illustrated hardcover. Recipes by women on the Board. See Dybwad and Bliss, bibliography citation #100, for illustration of the cover.

Valisi, G. *Chicago Day Waltz.* Chicago: Valisi, ^{c}1893. 4 *l.* Color cover lithograph by Orcutt Company (illustrated on page 2). Dedicated to Lena Burton Clarke, Chairman, Committee on Music, Board of Lady Managers.

White, Trumbull, and Wm. Igleheart. *The World's Columbian Exposition, Chicago, 1893. A Complete History of the Enterprise.* Boston: Gately, [^{c}1893]. 628 p., illustrated. General reference on the fair. Hunter's cabin, Choral Hall, and 1851 Crystal Palace illustrations.

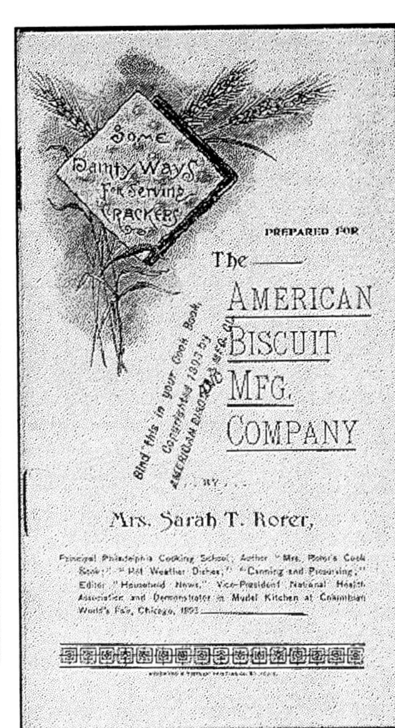

World's Columbian Exposition [Company]. *Concession Agreements.* Chicago: Chicago Legal News, 1893. 27½ x 21½. 3 p. agreement for the photography concession (illustrated on page 86). The Exposition owned the Photography Bureau and sold Arnold's and Higinbotham's photographs for publicity and income. In turn, the two received $2,000 per year salary and 10 percent of the net receipts of the Bureau. The Bureau licensed all cameras and stereo views.

World's Columbian Exposition [Company]. Department of Publicity and Promotion. *The Official Directory of the World's Columbian Exposition : May 1st to October 30th, 1893.* Ed. Moses P. Handy. Chicago: Conkey, 1893. vii, 1120 p., hardcover. This book not only lists the exhibitors by department but also contains an excellent history and organization of the Exposition. It does not contain a listing of any of the French exhibits.

The World's Columbian Exposition Reproduced. Chicago: Rand, 1894. 120 *l* of plates with captions, hardcover. Illustration of Hussars at evening parade and Baldwin's balloon ascension from Government Plaza on Chicago Day.

References for "Gas Ballooning in the Gay '90s" by Ruth Owen Jones:

Aeronautics. October 1893 monthly to September 1894. Special Collections, Frost Library, Amherst College, Amherst, MA. See general reference list above.

Chicago Daily Tribune. "Passes Above Crowd in a Balloon." October 10, 1893, page 1, column 4. Baldwin's ascent in the "General Myer" on Chicago Day, October 9, 1893.

Crouch, Tom D. *The Eagle Aloft: Two Centuries of the Balloon in America.* Washington, DC: Smithsonian Institution, 1983.

Emme, Eugene M. *Aeronautics and Astronautics.* Washington, DC: NASA, 1961.

Gilman, Rhoda R. "Balloon to Boston: Samuel A. King and the 'Great Northwest.'" *Minnesota History.* 42 (Spring 1970): 17-22.

Trimble, William F. *High Frontier: A History of Aeronautics in Pennsylvania.* Pittsburgh: U of Pittsburgh P, 1982. Describes Samuel F. King and his "Eagle Eyrie."

References for "Photography and Fairs" by Thomas Yanul:

Brown, Julie K. *Contesting Images.* See general reference list above.

Gourdon, Jean-Michel, ed. *Le Studio Chevojon - une Dynastie de Photographs Parisiens.* Paris: Maison de la Villette, 1994.

Image. Article by Julie K. Brown. See general reference list above.

McCauley, Elizabeth Anne. *Industrial Madness: Commercial Photography on Paris, 1848-1871.* New Haven, CT: Yale UP, 1994.

INDEX

J. C. Penney Photo

Joy V. Bliss, native of North Dakota, current resident of New Mexico, has degrees in chemistry, medicine, and law. A retired anesthesiologist, she enjoys research and writing, computers, photography, and traveling.

G. L. Dybwad, born and raised in North Dakota, graduated from the University of North Dakota and Kansas State University with a doctorate in physics. Past-president of an AT&T Bell Laboratories Camera Club and long time collector of World's Columbian Exposition memorabilia, since his retirement from Sandia National Laboratories, Albuquerque, he has enjoyed having more time for books: collecting and selling used books, archival repair, writing, and publishing.

About this book:

The text, "CG Times" 11-point, is printed on 80 pound sterling matte paper. Black-and-white and color halftones were produced with 150-line screens. The book is Smythe case sewn and bound in matte-film laminate covers.

The enclosed Heinze architectural map, originally color and 25 x 25 inches, was reproduced using a 200-line screen halftone with overlay printed in red. The map was printed on 60 pound enamel text.

Color separations and map prepress were generated by Southwest Electronic Prepress Services, Albuquerque, New Mexico, and the map was printed by Albuquerque Printing Company. BookCrafters, Chelsea, Michigan, produced all black-and-white text halftones and printed the book.